Somewhere In Heaven

OTHER BOOKS BY CHRISTOPHER ANDERSEN

After Diana

Barbra:
The Way She Is

American Evita:
Hillary Clinton's Path to Power

Sweet Caroline:
Last Child of Camelot

George and Laura:
Portrait of an American Marriage

Diana's Boys

The Day John Died

Bill and Hillary: The Marriage

The Day Diana Died

Jackie After Jack: Portrait of the Lady

An Affair to Remember

Jack and Jackie

Young Kate

Citizen Jane

The Best of Everything

The Serpent's Tooth

The Book of People

Father

The Name Game

Somewhere In Heaven

The Remarkable Story of
Dana and Christopher Reeve

CHRISTOPHER ANDERSEN

EBURY
PRESS

1 3 5 7 9 10 8 6 4 2

Published in 2008 by Ebury Press, an imprint of Ebury Publishing
A Random House Group Company
First Published in the United States by Hyperion in 2008

The Random House Group Limited Reg. No. 954009

Addresses for companies within the Random House Group can be found at
www.randomhouse.co.uk

A CIP catalogue record for this book is available from the British Library

The Random House Group Limited supports The Forest Stewardship Council (FSC),
the leading international forest certification organisation. All our titles that are printed on
Greenpeace approved FSC certified paper carry the FSC logo. Our paper procurement
policy can be found at www.rbooks.co.uk/environment

Mixed Sources
Product group from well-managed
forests and other controlled sources
www.fsc.org Cert no. TT-COC-2139
© 1996 Forest Stewardship Council

Printed and bound in Great Britain by Clays Ltd, St Ives PLC

ISBN 9780091927660

To buy books by your favourite authors and register for offers visit www.rbooks.co.uk

Grateful acknowledgment is made to the following for permission to reprint
the photographs in this book:

AP Photo: 30, 33; AP Photo/Robert F. Bukaty: 22; AP Photo/Steve
Helber: 17; AP Photo/Sandy Macys: 28; AP Photo/Elliot D. Novak: 16;
John Barrett/Globe Photos: 10, 14, 35; Berliner Studios/BEI: 20;
Black/Sail/Sipa: 21; Diane Cohen/Sipa: 24, 29; James Colburn/IPOL/Globe
Photos: 6; Globe Photos: 2, 5, 26; Kelly Jordan/Globe Photos: 1, 25;
Janet C. Koltick/Globe Photos: 19; Nina Kreiger/BEImages: 7, 8, 9;
John Krondes/Globe Photo: 34; MANTEL/Sipa Press: 18; Sonia
Moskowitz/Globe Photos: 27, 32; Adam Scull/Globe Photos: 11, 12, 13;
SN/Globe Photos: 23; Anita Weber/Sipa: 3, 4; West Wind L.P./
WireImage: 15; John Zissel/Globe Photos: 31

For those who never give up

CHRIS: Yes, we are lovers, and
I hope we always will be.
I will always be in love
with Dana.

DANA: And I will always be in love
with Chris.

"Real love, and the ability to love
somebody as damaged as I was,
that is a very rare and precious thing."
—*Chris*

"It was easy to fall in love with
him. He is extraordinary."
—*Dana*

"There are not that many times
when you come across that true,
shining love that Chris and Dana
had for each other."
—*Barbara Walters*

PREFACE

———

By any definition, they were a golden couple—young, talented, famous, rich, impossibly beautiful, disarmingly charming, and improbably down to earth. He had rocketed to international fame at age twenty-six wearing the red-and-yellow cape of America's greatest superhero. She was the aspiring singer-actress with the disarmingly self-deprecating wit who—at five feet seven inches to his six feet four inches—was nevertheless by any measure his equal.

The evidence of this perfect life they shared seemed to be everywhere. At glittering premieres and charity events, they always paused on the red carpet to smile politely for the cameras. They were socially conscious, politically engaged, and crusaded for the causes they believed in. Away from the spotlight, they were simply besotted with the young son they had together, and lavished no less affection on his two children from a previous relationship. They traveled among several homes in the private plane he piloted, and sailed the Northeastern coastline of the United States in their custom-built yacht. In public and in private, they embraced often and laughed even more. Clearly, they had every reason to.

Then it happened. In a horrifying instant, Christopher Reeve—the quintessential man of action both on and off screen—was at age forty-two rendered a wheelchair-bound quadriplegic, completely paralyzed from the shoulders down, unable even to breathe on his own. To the world, the life Chris and Dana had shared seemed irretrievably broken—shattered beyond all repair.

They were wrong. Over the next nine years, Chris, with Dana steadfastly at his side, would battle back to become both a leader in the fight to cure spinal cord injuries and a symbol of hope for millions. By the time he died suddenly and unexpectedly from an infection on October 10, 2004, Reeve was soaring higher as a humanitarian than he ever had on screen.

Chris's suffering was over, but not Dana's. Just four months later, Dana's beloved mother died unexpectedly after being operated on for ovarian cancer. Then Dana would wage her own war for survival with the same dignity, courage, and humor that were the hallmarks of her life with Chris. But she would face her own crisis bearing a burden that Chris never had to: the knowledge that Will, who had scarcely gotten over the passing of his dad and his grandmother, could soon be left an orphan.

The miracle Chris and Dana set out to achieve—the medical breakthrough that would have enabled him to walk again—has yet to happen. Yet what they *were* as a couple, before and after the accident that changed their lives forever, was nothing short of miraculous. Theirs was a saga of fate, faith, grace, and grit—a tale of triumph and tragedy, as inspiring as it was heartbreaking. Yet it was one thing above all others: a love story.

Somewhere In Heaven

"They were so close. How lucky they
were to have each other."

—*Michael J. Fox*

"You looked at the two of them
and you said to yourself, 'Man, this
is really something.'"

—*Edward Herrmann,*
actor and friend

1

Saturday, October 9, 2004
Backstage at Southcoast Repertory Theater
Costa Mesa, California

She was one of the bravest women Mimi Lieber had ever known. But when Lieber poked her head into the cramped dressing room to ask if Dana Reeve would be joining her and the rest of the cast of Broadway-bound *Brooklyn Boy* that night for a post-show drink, the solitary figure she saw was plainly terrified.

Dana had been on the road performing in *Brooklyn Boy* for two months—visiting home most weekends—and was set to fly back to New York once and for all the next day. She had spoken to Chris on the phone only a few hours before about how excited she was to finally be returning to her family. Now, in an instant, that excitement had turned to dread.

"Something's wrong at home," Dana explained, using one trembling hand to steady the other as she clasped the phone to her ear. While Dana had been onstage, one of her husband's physicians had left an urgent message on her cell phone. Dana had received many emergency calls like this in the nine years since Chris's accident, as he faced one medical crisis after another. But this time the doctor's tone was unmistakably ominous.

It had all happened with such alarming speed. Although Chris could not feel it, the bedsore on his lower back was of growing concern—this on top of the systemic infection he had been fighting for nearly three months. A powerful combination of what Reeve liked to call "industrial-strength" antibiotics had worked against these infections in the past, but he had built up a resistance to them over the years. Now the nurses who took care of Chris around the clock begged him to stay in bed so the drugs could take effect.

The patient had other ideas. With Dana twenty-six hundred miles away, Chris felt it was more important than ever that he attend their twelve-year-old son Will's peewee league hockey game that afternoon. Moreover, it was a key matchup: Will's team, the Westchester Express, was set to go head-to-head with their archrivals, the Mass Conn Braves from Springfield, Massachusetts.

Nonetheless, the nurses continued to plead with Chris. "Please stay home this one time . . . This doesn't look good."

"No, I'm going," Chris shot back.

"But you go to all of Will's games. You can miss one. He'll understand."

"No, no, no," Chris replied. "I want to watch Will play! So let's go!"

It took more than three hours for the aides to dress Reeve, load his wheelchair onto his specially outfitted van—"Every time we leave the house, it's a production," Dana liked to joke—and drive the twenty miles to the Brewster Ice Arena. But once the Westchester Express took to the ice at 3:20 P.M., Chris was at rink level behind the glass, cheering Will and his team on.

"*Will, Will, Will,*" Chris chanted as his son scored two of the Express's eleven goals to defeat the Braves. Will's winning moves earned him the game puck for the day.

By 6 P.M., father and son were back at home on Great Hills Farm Road in suburban Bedford, New York. While Will showered and then chatted with friends online, Chris placed a call to then–Democratic presidential nominee John Kerry. The Reeves had campaigned for Kerry, a strong supporter of stem cell research that might lead to a cure for spinal cord injuries, and Chris wanted to thank the Massachusetts senator for mentioning him by name during the most recent presidential debate. "Chris was very excited about the future," Kerry recalled. "It was a long conversation about all the things we wanted to accomplish. I knew he hadn't been feeling well, but he gave no indication that he was in distress. He was . . . exuberant."

Both ardent Yankee fans, Will and his dad dined on turkey tetrazzini while glued to the Yankees–Minnesota Twins game on television. They both cheered when the Yankees won. It had been a great day, Will later said, "for father-son bonding."

At around 10:30 P.M., Chris was in bed and Will dropped in to say good night. He switched the set to CNN so his father could watch the latest campaign coverage, and then said good night the way he always did: Will kissed his father on the forehead, then, as he was leaving, took Chris's big toe between his thumb and forefinger and wiggled it. It was the last time he saw his father conscious.

Will was already fast asleep when, shortly before midnight, his father suffered a massive heart attack. Chris was resuscitated and rushed by ambulance to Northern Westchester Hospital in nearby Mt. Kisco. Now Dana was being told over the phone that her husband was alive, but comatose.

"Do I need to get a plane right now?" Dana asked the doctor, her steady voice masking a rising panic.

"Yes, I think you do," he replied.

"Could he die?" Dana inquired point-blank.

"Yes."

She hesitated for a moment before asking one more question—the one that, in her mind, said more about the gravity of the situation than any other. It was a question that, even during the worst of the many crises that had gone before, none of Chris's doctors had ever said yes to.

"Do I . . . ," Dana asked. "Do I need to call the kids?"

"Yes."

Dana took a deep breath. She hung up the phone and immediately called the one person she knew who had the resources and the pull to get her a private jet on a moment's notice—Marsha Williams, wife of Chris's close pal Robin Williams.

Next, Dana phoned Will, who was now being looked after by family friends. "I'm coming home right now," she told Will. She tried to reassure him. "Don't worry too much. Dad's a tough guy—he's been through things like this before and bounced right back."

As she headed for Los Angeles Airport to board the private jet arranged by Marsha Williams, Dana worked her cell phone. She called London to discover that Matthew Reeve, one of two children from Chris's ten-year relationship with British modeling agent Gae Exton, was already on his way from England with his mother.

Meanwhile, Will's half-sister Alexandra, an undergraduate student at Yale, had driven down from New Haven. Within an hour of her father's arrival at the hospital, she was sitting at his bedside.

Alexandra had been warned that Chris had lapsed into a coma and was not responding to stimuli. But when she leaned in to speak to him, she noticed that his eyes "flickered. He knew I was there. He definitely heard me."

It was precisely the hopeful sign Dana needed. As she flew across the country, she checked in with Alexandra, who reassured her that Chris was sleeping peacefully through the night. There had been emergencies like this in the past, Dana told herself—times when he'd been rushed off to the hospital, and yet he'd always somehow managed to come through. "I thought," she later confessed, "*There's a possibility . . .*"

Hope faded in the early morning hours of October 10, however, when Chris suffered a series of cardiac arrests. Each time, intensive care doctors fought frantically to pull him back from the brink—all in keeping with Dana's wishes. "Please, please," Dana told doctors from the plane. "Just keep him alive until I get there."

By the time Dana arrived at Westchester County Airport late

that afternoon, most of the family was already at the hospital. Gae Exton and Matthew were there from London, as were Chris's father, Franklin Reeve, his brother Benjamin, and Dana's parents.

Chris's mother, Barbara, an angular, athletic woman who enjoyed rowing on Boston's Charles River well into her seventies, had received a call at 7:30 A.M. that Chris was in intensive care and driven two hours from her home in Princeton, New Jersey. When Chris suffered his famous horseback riding accident nine years earlier, it was Barbara who stood over his bed at the University of Virginia Medical Center and made the case for taking her son off life support. "All I could think of was how active he was—sailing, scuba diving, flying a plane, skiing, tennis," she later recalled. "I didn't feel he would want to live if he was paralyzed, trapped in his own body."

Although she risked angering Dana and the rest of the family back in June of 1995, Chris's mother had persisted. "I just don't understand," she told the others, "why we are doing all these measures just to keep him alive." It's not, she said, "the kind of life he would want to live."

At the time, Barbara's son by her second marriage, Chris's half-brother Jeffrey, took her aside. "Mom, Chris would want to be able to see Will grow up," Jeff said of the then-three-year-old boy, "even out of the corner of his eye." It was then, Barbara admitted, that she finally "came around" to the idea that life as a quadriplegic was still worth living.

The ventilators and monitors were still whooshing and beeping as they kept Chris alive, but this time things were different and everyone in the room knew it. As her son neared the end of his life, Barbara leaned over and whispered in his ear. "You're free,

Chris," she said. "You fought a good fight and now you are finally *free*, Chris. You're free of all these tubes!"

When she got to the hospital, Dana didn't wait for the elevator. Instead, she dashed up the stairs to the second floor, threw her things down, and ran into Chris's room. "The good news," Mimi Lieber later observed, "is that Dana made it. I think he waited for her."

Now that she was finally on the scene and able to help her son through this terrible ordeal, Dana asked for Will to be driven to the hospital. Once he got there, Dana fought the urge to break down as she wrapped him up in her arms. "We're going to say good-bye to Dad now," she whispered into his ear. Then, taking his hand, Dana led Will into intensive care.

Chris had never emerged from his coma, but Will believed that somehow he knew the people who loved him were there. Will softly kissed his father on the forehead and gently wiggled Chris's toe.

"Night, Dad," Will said.

"Funny how love just sort of
—sneaks up on you."
—*Dana*

"Dana knows every corner of me."
—*Chris*

2

June 30, 1987
Williamstown, Massachusetts

He simply could not take his eyes off her. Wearing a short black off-the-shoulder evening dress, her auburn hair tumbling over tanned shoulders, Dana Morosini confidently took the microphone off the stand and gazed through the blue haze of cigarette smoke out over the heads of those sitting ringside. Then, in a sweet mezzo-soprano, she eased into Jule Styne's lyrical ballad "The Music That Makes Me Dance."

Williamstown was, in many ways, home to Christopher Reeve. It was here, at the annual theater festival held on the campus of Williams College, that Chris had come every summer since 1968 to sharpen his skills as a stage actor. As he had also done every year since 1968, Chris—cast this season in Aphra Behn's costume drama *The Rover*—after a hard day's rehearsal unwound with his fellow actors at the 1896 House, a quaint white-clapboard country inn nestled in the Berkshire hills.

Each night during the summer, festival-goers packed the inn's dimly lit, ground-floor cabaret—often in hopes of seeing one of the stars perform. Over the years Chris had gamely obliged, summoning enough courage to take the stage and belt out numbers by Cole Porter, Rodgers and Hammerstein, and the Gershwins. "A lot of us have no business singing," he allowed, "but the crowd seems to get a kick out of it."

Tonight, however, Chris was content to sit back and listen to the Cabaret Corps, the tight little group of four professional singers who took up the slack each evening. Reeve's friends nudged one another as he kept staring at the slender young singer with the enormous eyes and blinding smile. Chris was oblivious to everything in the room—the clinking glasses, the hum of table conversation punctuated by clattering sounds from the kitchen, and the occasional spike of laughter—everything but Dana.

POW! BIFF! "That was it," Chris later said. "Right then I went down hook, line, and sinker. She just knocked me out. A lot of people saw that happen." The inn's co-owner, Denise Richer, was one of them. "We kept looking at the stage, and then at him, and then back at her," Richer said, "and we thought, 'Something's happening here.' It was so obvious." According to fellow *Rover* cast member Charles Tuthill, who was standing against the back wall with Chris, "he was totally hit between the eyes. She took his breath away."

When her number was over, Chris shook his head in wonder. "My God," he told his buddies, "who's *that*? She is incredible!"

As intently as Chris had been staring at Dana, she had been doing her best to ignore his presence in the audience. It had been eight years since he shot to stardom as the Man of Steel, and with three sequels under his yellow belt, Reeve and the iconic comic book hero he portrayed on screen now seemed virtually inseparable. If anything, at thirty-five Reeve now seemed more physically striking than ever. Standing a full head taller than virtually everyone else in the room and decked out in his customary preppie uniform of pale blue polo shirt, khakis, and Docksiders without socks, Chris was impossible to miss. "I just pretended Superman wasn't there," she recalled wryly. "Not as easy as it sounds."

She had her reasons. That summer Reeve's breakup with Gae Exton, his girlfriend of ten years and the mother of his two children, was grist for the rumor mill. While shooting *Superman IV* in London a few months earlier, he had been romantically linked with leading lady Mariel Hemingway. Now Williamstown was abuzz with gossip that Chris was on the prowl.

Afterward, Chris went backstage to congratulate the woman who had, it would turn out, won his heart with a single song. "Hi, I'm Chris Reeve," he said with all the awkward charm of Clark Kent.

"Yes," she replied, stifling the urge to blurt out, "You must be kidding." Still suspicious of his motives—her friends had warned her he was in the audience and on the make only moments before she stepped onstage—she politely introduced herself in return, and then listened as he heaped praise on her performance.

"I've always liked that song," said Chris, who sheepishly admitted to being a fan of Broadway musicals in general and *Funny Girl* in particular. "It's a great song," he told her. "You know," he went on, struggling to make small talk, "Streisand loved that song, but they cut it from the movie."

"I know." She nodded, trying not to appear surprised that one of the biggest action stars of the decade not only liked show tunes but was a Barbra Streisand fan. Maybe he wasn't going to make a move on her, she thought. Maybe her friends were completely wrong about Reeve and his intentions.

They were right, as it turned out. Chris and a few of his fellow actors from the cast of *The Rover* were headed to The Zoo, an after-hours *Animal House*–style hangout tucked away in a dormitory on the Williams College campus. The name of the establishment said it all.

"Would you like a ride?" he asked. "My truck is parked right outside."

"Oh, no," Dana replied without missing a beat as several of her friends showed up to congratulate her. "That's OK. I've got my own car."

"Oh," Chris mumbled as she disappeared in the crowd. This was not the kind of response Superman was accustomed to.

Dana, meantime, was being scolded by pals who had witnessed Chris's timid overtures. "You are *crazy*," one chided her. "Why don't you go with him?"

"But I *have* a car," she insisted. "I can get there on my own."

"Give us your keys right now!" one demanded. "We'll drive your damn car. Christopher Reeve wants to give you a ride. Now go for it!"

"But why would I leave my perfectly good car in the parking lot," Dana persisted stubbornly, "and then be stuck at the party?"

Her friends rolled their eyes, but by then it was too late; Chris had already spun out of the parking lot behind the wheel of his battered black pickup, hoping to meet up with Dana at The Zoo. When he got there, he ignored his friends and did not even bother to stop at the bar. Instead he stood where he could get a clear view of the front door, hands thrust in his pockets, waiting for the beautiful girl in the black off-the-shoulder dress to walk in.

Dana arrived a few minutes later, and scanned the crowd for Chris. Their eyes locked, and within moments they were standing together in the center of the crammed room. He had strolled up to her with a studied nonchalance that she found disarmingly clumsy. "Could I get you a drink?" he asked, and she said sure. But he never did. "We didn't get a drink, we didn't sit down, we didn't move," he later said. For the next hour, everything and everyone around them melted away as they stood talking—just talking.

Don't rush this, Chris told himself. *It's too important . . .*

"Well," he blurted as he looked at his watch. "It's getting late . . . It was very nice to meet you." She, in turn, shook his hand, and a half hour later both were back home in their own beds.

They would eventually call June 30, 1987, simply "our day." But on this, the day they met, they were each privately asking the same thing: "Do I really want to do this?"

At that point in their lives, Chris and Dana both had reasons for walking—running—in opposite directions. At twenty-six, Dana was making her Williamstown debut doing supporting parts on-stage, then, once the curtain fell, rushing to the 1896 House to belt out numbers as one of the Cabaret Corps. The Williamstown Festival, which for years had attracted major stars like Chris yearning to reconnect with their roots in live theater, had also long been regarded as a showcase for up-and-coming talent. Dana Charles Morosini needed the work, and she needed to land that all-important break.

Not that she had ever faced any real hardships in her early life—far from it. Dana was born on March 17, 1961, in suburban Teaneck, New Jersey. Her father, Charles (who provided Dana with her gender-bending middle name), was a respected cardiologist, while mom, Helen, worked for a New York publishing house.

When Dana was a child, the Morosinis moved to Greenburgh, New York, a decidedly more upscale commuter enclave in country club–speckled Westchester County. All three Morosini daughters were excellent students, eager to please their demanding dad. "These were very capable young ladies," said one family friend. "They could do anything a boy could—and that included chopping firewood." (Eldest sister Deborah would wind up following in Daddy's footsteps by becoming a noted physician and medical researcher, while baby of the family Adrienne became a successful real estate agent.)

In this family of headstrong achievers, Dana took on the classic role of the middle child. Whenever the inevitable family squabbles took place, it was Dana who calmed the waters. "She was the nurturer, the peacekeeper," Adrienne said.

"She was outgoing and lots of fun and good at everything she did," said a childhood friend. "But she was also very conscious, even at a young age, of not hurting people's feelings. If it looked like another kid was being ganged up on or excluded for some reason, she always came to their rescue."

Dana also had a vivid imagination. She not only walked down the street holding the hand of her imaginary friend, but also could picture her imaginary friend's imaginary hat. "I had a very rich fantasy life," she later recalled. "I liked to pretend, to invent characters and situations, like practically everybody who winds up becoming an actor."

Like multitudes of other American girls, Dana also became fascinated with horses, and before she was seven she was riding competitively at equestrian centers in New Jersey and Westchester County. "Like everything else she did," her mother once said, "Dana threw her whole heart and soul into doing it right. She had great style and control, and she loved it. Dana really became a superb horsewoman."

Indeed, Dana was, said one family friend, "very spirited, and whatever she tried—tennis, skiing, track—she did fairly well." A sport at which Dana did not excel just happened to be one of her father's favorite pastimes. Charles Morosini had repeatedly tried to teach all three of his daughters how to sail on Long Island Sound, but, he said, "none of them quite got the hang of it."

At Greenburgh's Edgemont High, Dana was soon starring in nearly every school play and musical while at the same time maintaining a straight-A average. "Everybody was very impressed with Dana's singing," recalled one classmate, "but whenever you complimented her, she just laughed it off. She wasn't stuck up at all, and she wasn't afraid to make fun of herself. Students, teachers, parents—everybody loved her." One of the teachers at Edgemont,

Richard Glass, described Dana as being "a born leader, pure and simple." Accordingly, she was elected senior class president and, when she graduated in 1979, was voted "most admired" by her classmates.

Determined to pursue an acting career, Dana went to New York that summer following graduation to study with Nikos Psacharopoulos, the flamboyantly eccentric director and acting coach. A decade earlier, Psacharopoulos, who was also artistic director at Williamstown, had taken a teenage Christopher Reeve under his wing.

Dana also studied for a semester at the HB (for Herbert Berghof) Studio in Manhattan, where she was taught by Uta Hagen. The legendary stage actress was "brilliant, stern, and unrelenting," remembered Dana, who quickly learned that it was "a long, long way from being able to sing loud enough so that the parents in high school can hear you to acquiring the tools of acting."

Over the next four years, she would major in English Literature at Vermont's Middlebury College. But Dana would never abandon her dreams of a life on the stage. She took large roles in several college productions, including the part of the villainous Nurse Ratched in *One Flew Over the Cuckoo's Nest*. "Talk about casting against type," said fellow student Peter Kiernan, who later became one of the Reeves' closest friends and confidants. Coincidentally, Kiernan had grown up playing hockey with Chris. "Nurse Ratched is such a cold, awful character. Dana had to be a great actress to pull that off. She was such a warm, sweet, funny person—a beautiful human being, inside and out.

"Besides," Kiernan added, "can you imagine Dana stepping out

onstage in a skintight nurse's uniform? I could barely breathe." At
the time, Kiernan said, he was "totally smitten with her. She was
a knockout. I tried three or four times, but she would have nothing to do with me." (Twenty years later, he would bring up the
incident while introducing Dana to a group of movers and shakers at New York's Algonquin Hotel. "She turned beet red," Kiernan said. "She'd completely forgotten that I was the annoying guy
who kept hitting on her back in college. Not that I was the only
one, of course. She was gorgeous. Every guy felt the way I did.")

Determined to become an actress, Dana spent her junior year
abroad studying at the Royal Academy of Dramatic Art in London. After she graduated cum laude from Middlebury, Dana
headed off to Los Angeles to earn a master's of Fine Arts degree
from the West Coast's answer to Juilliard, the prestigious California Institute of the Arts.

Through it all, Dana apparently never had a committed, long-
term relationship. "A lot of guys were after her, of course," said one
of Dana's college friends, "and she certainly dated a few of them.
But Dana was too focused on her career to really get involved with
anybody who didn't knock her off her feet."

In 1986, Dana returned to New York to start auditioning. She
waited tables like every other aspiring actor, but there were also
small parts off-Broadway and off-off-Broadway, as well as work in
children's theater, regional theater, and the occasional singing gig.

For a lifelong nonsmoker, the nights spent belting out show
tunes and standards in hotel lobbies and dingy bars packed with
chain-smokers took their toll. By the time her last set was over,
Dana's eyes would be burning, her throat would feel dry and sore,
and she would often be fighting off waves of nausea. She could

hardly wait to get home to wash the smoky smell out of her clothes and her hair. "As bad as it is for me," Dana said, "imagine how awful it is for the people who have to wait on tables or tend bar for eight hours at a stretch. I feel so sorry for them."

She would never, by contrast, feel sorry for herself. "Dana was unbelievably positive and upbeat," Ed Herrmann said. "It sounds corny, but she was that proverbial person who lights up a room." Added a fellow struggling actor, "Dana never made a science of whining like the rest of us. But she was no Pollyanna, either. She felt the sting of rejection and disappointment as much as the rest of us did."

At audition after audition, she kept being passed over in favor of more seasoned actresses. "She comes across as the girl next door," Psacharopoulos observed, "at a time in the theater when they aren't always looking for the girl next door." When one scene called for her to cut loose with profanity, the casting director rejected her on the grounds that "nobody's going to believe words like that coming out of her mouth."

Little did they know. "Dana was a class act, but she was no prude," said a former member of Williamstown's Cabaret Corps. "When it was called for, she could swear with the best of them."

For the first time, cracks were beginning to show in Dana's facade of unbridled optimism. "It just wasn't happening," she allowed. "Of course, I was terribly frustrated. I just wanted the chance to show people what I was capable of as a performer."

So when Nikos Psacharopoulos invited her to be part of the Williamstown Festival's 1987 summer season (at a staggering salary of $25 per week), Dana pounced at the chance. She would be completely focused on her work to the exclusion of all else—

including men. The last thing she needed, Dana Morosini tried to convince herself, was the distraction of a summer romance. "I'm not in the market for some guy on the make," she confided to one of the other actresses at Williamstown. "I don't care *how* cute he is."

Like Dana, Chris was standing at a crossroads. His one long-term relationship had already crashed noisily to earth, and now his career seemed to be in a free fall.

Not that Reeve's life was ever as charmed as it seemed from the outside. A descendant of France's noble D'Olier clan, Chris's great-grandfather Franklin D'Olier became the president of the Prudential Insurance Company during the 1940s and would remain at the helm of Prudential for more than a quarter century. His grandson Franklin D'Olier Reeve decided to break away from the constraints of wealth and privilege—although not before allowing his family to pay his way through Princeton.

It was while pursuing a graduate degree in Russian Studies at Columbia—and flirting with socialism on the side—that Franklin Reeve met Vassar student Barbara Pitney Lamb at a family gathering. As it happened, Barbara Lamb's uncle had married Franklin's mother, Anne, after Anne divorced Franklin's father, Richard Reeve. It was just one small corner in the tangled web of divorces, remarriages, stepparents, half siblings, and stepsiblings that characterized the Family Reeve—and led to Chris's abiding distrust of marriage as an institution.

Barbara and Franklin ("F.D.") were married in 1951, and ten months later—on September 25, 1952—Christopher D'Olier

Reeve was born at Lenox Hill Hospital on New York's Upper East Side. A year later, Chris's brother Benjamin arrived. Despite the trappings of wealth—the D'Olier millions meant that all the Reeves would have entrée into the most elite prep schools, universities, and private clubs—"Tophy" and "Beejy" felt anything but secure growing up.

As tall, movie star–handsome F.D. climbed the ladder of academia to prominence as a translator, poet, and essayist, college-educated Barbara languished at home in the classic 1950s role of stay-at-home mom. The marriage soon unraveled, and by the time Chris was three his parents were divorced.

The boys, who went to live with their mother in Princeton, New Jersey, were never quite sure where they stood with their mercurial dad. After he married Columbia graduate student Helen Schmidinger in 1956, F.D. became less and less involved in his sons' lives, focusing instead on the three children he had with his new wife: Chris's half sister Alison ("Alya") and half brothers Brock and Mark.

The tension between Franklin and his first two boys became even more pronounced after Barbara married wealthy investment banker Tristram Johnson in 1959. The bluff, unrepentantly nonintellectual "Tris" brought his four children from a previous marriage—Johnny, Tommy, Beth, and Kate—into the mix, and by 1963 Chris had two new half brothers, Jeff and Kevin. Fun-loving and, unlike Franklin, decidedly down to earth, Tris Johnson was a generous and loving stepfather to Chris and Ben—so much so that Chris actively considered changing his surname to Johnson.

According to Chris, that bond may have made F.D. even more

resentful. Soon the boys were spending almost no time at all with their father. When he did return from the occasional weekend with Chris and Ben, Franklin deposited them a block away and ordered them to walk the rest of the way home. "I have no interest," he would snarl, "in seeing *that woman* or her new husband ever again."

No matter. Eventually, these second marriages would also end in divorce. "It did not exactly inspire confidence," Chris would later say, "in the ability of men and women to have any sort of lasting relationship at all."

Meanwhile, Chris and his brother were shuttled among Reeve and Johnson family homes in Princeton (where Mom landed a job as a reporter for the weekly *Town Topics*), Connecticut, Martha's Vineyard, and on the Jersey shore. Ironically, the boy who would grow up to play Superman was a sickly child. Like his mother, Chris was asthmatic and suffered from a wide range of allergies—including one to horses. He also suffered from Osgood-Schlatter disease, a painful medical condition which caused fluid to build up in the joints, and from alopecia; at periodic intervals and without any warning, his hair simply fell out by the handful. Nobody knew why.

None of this, however, kept Chris from being the classic first-born overachiever. He excelled in the classroom and—despite the grab bag of ailments that afflicted him—quickly proved himself to be a gifted athlete. A self-described loner, Chris preferred solitary pursuits like running, swimming, tennis, and fencing to team sports—a reflection of his own reluctance to depend on anyone else. (Chris would earn his varsity prep school letter in hockey, playing the more solitary position of goalie.)

Chris was also a gifted musician who practiced piano ninety minutes a day and, seemingly effortlessly, mastered elaborate pieces by Mozart, Ravel, and Debussy. Barbara Johnson would reward her son by giving him a Steinway Grand for his sixteenth birthday.

Chris also came to the realization at an early age that he could act. From the age of thirteen on, he would dash from school to the McCarter Theatre in Princeton, searching for any roles that called for an adolescent. Two years after joining the McCarter, he would be accepted by the Williamstown Theatre Festival, where he would return every subsequent summer—even after he struck gold in Hollywood. (By the time he met Dana, Chris had even built a beautiful hilltop home in Williamstown.)

In fact, the theater became his family. "I knew I was loved as a child," Chris said, "but I grew up feeling that I could not count on other people to always be there for me." In stark contrast to the stable and supportive family life Dana had enjoyed, Chris described his family as "all just bits and pieces. You don't want to risk getting involved with people for fear that things are going to fall apart. That's why I found relief in playing characters," continued Chris, who had an Actors' Equity Card at sixteen. "You knew where you were in fiction. You knew where you stood."

Even at age nineteen, Chris so impressed stage veterans that they eagerly cast him in a variety of parts. "In walked this gawky, earnest, slightly goofy Adonis," recalled Tony Award–winning director Jack O'Brien, "and yet what instantly struck you was his *mind*. He was so obviously, incredibly, bright."

By the time Chris graduated from Cornell University with a degree in English and Music Theory in 1974, he had apprenticed in summer stock, off-Broadway, and in regional theater. At the

Loeb Drama Center in Cambridge, Massachusetts, he played in everything from Turgenev's *A Month in the Country* to *Death of a Salesman*. He also played Macheath in the Manhattan Theater Club production of *The Threepenny Opera,* and acted opposite Oscar-winner Celeste Holm in *The Irregular Verb to Love* before being cast to play Eleanor Parker's much-younger lover in the comedy *Forty Carats*. (During that run, Chris experienced one of his many brushes with death when a fifty-pound spotlight crashed down onto the stage in the middle of a performance.)

From Cornell, Chris, with Jack O'Brien's help, enrolled at Juilliard to study under John Houseman, the curmudgeonly theater legend who won an Academy Award playing a crusty law professor in *The Paper Chase* but was best known for his Smith Barney TV commercials ("They make money the old-fashioned way. They *earn* it."). "Mr. Reeve, it's very important that you become a serious actor," Houseman intoned. "Unless, of course, they offer you a shitload of money to do something else."

That year at Juilliard, Chris studied with the likes of Kevin Kline, Mandy Patinkin, and William Hurt. But the friendship he began with his frenetic young roommate ("He was like a balloon that had been inflated and immediately released.") would last a lifetime. "We clicked right away because we were exact opposites," Chris later explained of his relationship with Robin Williams. Indeed, the stalwart uberpreppie seemed the perfect foil for Williams's crazed antics. "I never tried to top him—of course I couldn't. I never tried to do bits with him. I was just my old boring self."

To the fans of *Love of Life,* Chris was anything but boring. Heeding John Houseman's advice to go for the money, he dropped out of Juilliard to play bigamist tennis bum Ben Harper in the long-running CBS soap opera. Over the course of two years, Chris became one of the genre's most loved/hated cads—and brought himself the kind of fame that made him irresistible to, in his words, "a certain kind of scoundrel-loving woman." However artless his passes may have seemed, at twenty-three Chris took advantage of Manhattan's pre-AIDS singles scene. However, waking up in the morning next to someone he didn't know soon became, Chris said, "embarrassing and vaguely disappointing."

At the height of his soap opera fame, Chris got his shot at Broadway playing Katharine Hepburn's grandson in Enid Bagnold's *A Matter of Gravity*. As she always did when she met someone for the first time, Kate went out of her way to say something provocative, confrontational, or downright rude. When Chris brought greetings from his grandmother Beatrice Lamb, a former classmate of Hepburn's at Bryn Mawr, Kate replied, "Oh, Bea. I never could stand her." Then she sized Chris up head to toe, glared at his feet, and ordered him to shine his shoes.

During the endless rehearsals and out-of-town tryouts that followed, Chris refused to be cowed by the domineering Hepburn. She, in turn, developed an almost grandmotherly affection for him. At one point Chris, who was still flying back from tryouts in Philadelphia, Washington, New Haven, Boston, and Toronto to tape *Love of Life* in New York, collapsed onstage from exhaustion and malnutrition. Hepburn turned to the audience and joked, "This boy's a goddamn fool. He doesn't eat enough red meat!"

A Matter of Gravity received a lukewarm reception from critics, but the chance to see Hepburn onstage was enough to fill the theater for two and a half months. Chris even seized the opportunity to do a little family fence-mending on opening night. "I said, 'What the hell,' and got my parents and stepparents tickets all together in the same row," he remembered. By the time the curtain fell, the squabbling ex-spouses and their new mates had all "buried the hatchet."

Hepburn, for one, was impressed. "I come from a big family and I know from experience how impossibly pigheaded and stubborn one's relatives can be," she said. "It took guts to do what he did." From then on, Hepburn would be one of Christopher Reeve's biggest boosters—to the point of calling up studios to lobby on his behalf. "Chris is so honest, so genuine," she told one journalist at the time. "I wonder if maybe he's a little *too* good-looking. They really like to put ugly people in pictures these days. My God, just look at the creatures up there on the screen! But they're going to have to start putting attractive people back in the movies eventually . . . and once he finds the right part—a big, fat, juicy leading man part, I mean—Chris is going to be a big, big star."

Unfortunately, Chris made his film debut the following year playing a member of a nuclear submarine crew in *Gray Lady Down,* starring Charlton Heston. The movie sank at the box office. "I absolutely wrote myself off," said Chris, who spent the next five months "sponging off friends, sleeping on couches, turning into a vegetable, and then one day I said this isn't right."

Chris soon found himself back in New York, scrambling for anything he could get. He had just been turned down for a Woolite commercial when the call came that would change his life forever.

When Chris told his father that he had been chosen out of a field that at one time or another had included Steve McQueen,

Robert Redford, James Caan, Bruce Jenner, and Sylvester Stallone to star in a big budget screen version of *Superman,* F.D. was ecstatic—until it dawned on him that Chris was not talking about the lead in George Bernard Shaw's *Man and Superman.* When Chris mentioned that the producers had not yet cast the role of Lois Lane, F.D. looked visibly deflated. "Oh," he said archly, "*that* Superman."

Growing up among such bookish Ivy Leaguers, Chris was only vaguely aware of Superman and never watched the highly successful 1950s TV serial starring George Reeves. As an aficionado of Hollywood lore, however, Chris was aware that Reeves, whose surname so closely resembled his own, grew despondent over being typecast as Superman and shot himself to death in 1959.

"I haven't been acting this long to be typecast as Superman," said Chris, shrugging off the notion of a Superman curse. "Once this movie is out, I'll play neurotics or weaklings. But right now Superman is not a bad role for me."

Chris actually had his doubts, and sought advice from friends. "It's so big and it's so scary," he told Jack O'Brien. "I'm afraid of what it might do to me."

"You have a great mind," O'Brien told him. "You won't lose your way, Chris. You won't lose yourself—I promise you."

Chris attacked the job the way he did everything else in life— with a single-minded ferocity. By way of transforming his athletic but slender physique, he spent at least four hours a day lifting weights for ten weeks, packing thirty-three pounds of muscle onto his six-foot-four-inch frame. He also proved himself more than capable of playing Superman's alter ego, the stoop-shouldered, bespectacled, lovably shy Clark Kent. By the time he went before the cameras in London, it looked as if Chris had stepped right out of the pages of the comic book. "If there's a God in heaven," said *Superman* director Richard Donner, "he sent me Christopher Reeve."

Chris, who had earned his pilot's license in his spare time and was flying his single-engine A36 Bonanza whenever and wherever he could, was also insisting on doing his own stunts in the movie. Dangling from wires for hours on end, he worked for hours perfecting his takeoffs and landings as the Man of Steel. Marlon Brando, who played Superman's father, Jor-El, tried to talk Reeve out of taking any unnecessary chances. "Why risk your neck?" Brando asked. "It's only a movie."

Released in December of 1978, *Superman* was an instant smash. The film would go on to gross more than $300 million worldwide—five times its production budget—in the process making it one of the biggest moneymakers of all time and Chris the proverbial overnight star. He admitted to being "a little overwhelmed" by how strongly the public identified him with the quintessentially American icon he was portraying.

"You would not believe," Chris told one writer, "what women would expect from somebody who played Superman." There would be hundreds of overtures and propositions, but Chris was no longer available. Months earlier, Chris was on the commissary lunch line during the shooting of *Superman* when he backed up and accidentally stepped on the foot of modeling agent Gae Exton. While it was hardly love at first sight for the leggy, blond Exton, Chris was instantly smitten.

Fresh from a bitter breakup with her millionaire husband, David Iverson, Exton kept Chris at arm's length until the third date. Even then, all they did was kiss. "She was shocked," he recalled, "that I wasn't going to muscle past the door into her bed."

Things moved rather quickly from then on. After months

during which the tabloids linked the hunky Reeve with every-body from his *Superman* costar Valerie Perrine to Farrah Fawcett, Chris appeared with Exton at the film's royal premiere in London.

Not all of Reeve's fans were beautiful, high-profile women. Chris would occasionally slip into his red cape, black boots, and blue tights and make surprise visits to children's hospitals and pe-diatric wards. Through the Make-A-Wish Foundation, he also fulfilled the dying wishes of several terminally ill children to meet Superman. "It's very hard for me to be silly about Superman," Reeve said, "because I have seen children dying of brain tumors who as their last request wanted to talk to me, and have gone to their graves with a kind of peace . . . I've seen that Superman really matters."

Financially, Superman mattered less to Chris than it did to sev-eral supporting players. While Brando took home $3.7 million for a few days' work and Gene Hackman collected $2 million playing Superman's nemesis Lex Luthor, Chris was paid a mere $250,000 for both the original *and* the sequel.

Nevertheless, the film vaulted Reeve from the ranks of jour-neyman soap stars to Hollywood's A List of leading men. Soon multimillion-dollar offers were pouring in. In quick succession, Chris turned down the racy *American Gigolo* (the movie would help turn Richard Gere into a star), the even racier *Body Heat* (a career-maker for William Hurt), and the part of Fletcher Chris-tian in a big budget remake of *Mutiny on the Bounty* (the part went to up-and-comer Mel Gibson).

Vowing to "escape the cape," Chris chose a low-budget time-travel romance as his next project. The movie would be released to lackluster reviews and fail at the box office. But over the years,

Somewhere in Time would, like such initial box office flops as *The Wizard of Oz* and *It's a Wonderful Life,* go on to develop a huge following. (The film would also have immense international appeal. *Somewhere in Time* was an immediate hit when it was released in Asia in 1984; the movie wound up playing before packed houses at Hong Kong's Palace Theater for eighteen months straight. By 2008, *Somewhere in Time* would rank as the sixth highest-grossing film of all time in China. Back in the U.S., the film would air countless times on television to strong ratings, spawning the International Network of *Somewhere in Time* Enthusiasts (INSITE), several Internet Web sites, and a cottage industry of books, posters, photographs, CDs, DVDs, and movie-related memorabilia.)

Chris's love interest in the film was British actress Jane Seymour, a onetime Bond girl (she played Solitaire opposite Roger Moore as 007 in *Live and Let Die*) who would go on to star in the hit CBS series *Dr. Quinn, Medicine Woman.* In *Somewhere in Time,* Chris plays a young writer who falls in love with the portrait of a long-dead actress (Seymour) and journeys back in time to meet her. "I was surprised and delighted that Chris wanted the part," said Richard Matheson, on whose book *Bid Time Return Somewhere in Time* was based. "He approached it perfectly, bringing an honesty and an innocence to his character that is tremendously appealing to audiences—to men as well as women."

For Chris, the film posed more than just an acting challenge. More than any other screen project, *Somewhere in Time* wreaked havoc with his allergy to horses. The movie was shot in and around the Grand Hotel on Michigan's picturesque Mackinac Island, where all cars were banned. Horse-drawn carriages were the only mode of transportation allowed, which meant there were nearly seven hundred horses roaming the island at any given time. Even though he was doubling up on his allergy medication, Chris occasionally succumbed to an attack. While the crew waited to begin, the star put drops in his eyes to keep them from watering and waited for the coughing and wheezing to subside.

Stung by *Somewhere in Time*'s initially cool reception (the *New York Times*'s Vincent Canby described Reeve as looking and sounding like a "helium-filled canary" in the film), Chris returned to London with Exton to finish *Superman II*. It was there that Matthew Exton Reeve was born on December 20, 1979, at the Welbeck Street Clinic in Mayfair. The baby's arrival taught Chris that "unconditional love is everything." But it did not convince him that it was time to marry Matthew's mother. Gae did not press the issue, although she drew the line at more children without matrimony. "One illegitimate child is fine," she allowed, "but two, is, well, tacky."

Surprisingly, *Superman II* met with both critical acclaim and success at the box office—one of the few sequels that equaled or, in the view of many, surpassed the original. Reeve would later say he felt that it was the best of the series.

Not surprisingly, Chris was now more closely identified than ever with the superhero he brought to life on screen. Still determined to escape the cape, he went back to Broadway, this time playing a Vietnam veteran whose legs had been blown off by a land mine in Lanford Wilson's searing drama *Fifth of July*. In researching the role at a Brooklyn Veterans Administration hospital, Chris was given his first real glimpse into the challenges faced by the disabled.

Chris followed *Fifth of July* up by taking on the role of Michael Caine's psychopathic lover in Sidney Lumet's *Deathtrap*. But in 1982, Reeve was persuaded by director Richard Lester to don the cape once again for *Superman III*. It was while filming this latest episode in the Superman saga that Chris decided to take a hot air balloon ride with his longtime friend, photographer Ken Regan. "My contract says that while I'm making *Superman,* I can't fly my plane," Reeve explained, "but it doesn't say anything about a balloon!"

As it turned out, they got off to a late start and wound up landing after dark—directly on a tree stump in an open field. Both men were jettisoned from the basket on impact. Regan managed to struggle to his feet and called out Chris's name in the darkness. Nothing. "Oh no, I've killed Superman!" Regan thought to himself. Finally, he heard his friend moaning. "Oh, God," he said, "I think I broke everything in my body." Regan rushed up to help Chris, who was sprawled out on the grass. When he got there and knelt down, his friend burst out laughing. "I could have slugged him," Regan later recalled. "He was absolutely fine."

As soon as *Superman III* was completed, Chris wasted no time again trying to distance himself from the role that had made him famous. The anti-Superman crusade continued with Merchant Ivory's *The Bostonians,* in which Chris was cast as impoverished writer Basil Ransome. Later, while playing a barnstorming air-mail pilot in *The Aviator* (for which the thrill-seeking Chris did his own aerial stunts), Chris became a father a second time with the arrival of Alexandra Exton Reeve in December of 1983. Holding to the conviction that "in most cases marriage is a sham," Chris made it clear that he still had no intention of tying the knot with Gae—no matter how "tacky" it was to have two illegitimate children.

As devoted as he undoubtedly was to Matthew and Alexandra, the fact remained that Chris was essentially an absent father. When he wasn't poring over scripts, acting on the stage, or away on a film location, Chris was crisscrossing the country (or flying solo across the Atlantic) at the controls of his new twin-engine Beechcraft, skiing down some of the world's most challenging runs, or soaring over mountaintops in his glider. Reeve was also, he would later admit, seeing other women—lots of other women. He conceded that the pressures of fatherhood and family during this period made him feel "unsettled and restless."

The more "restless" he felt, the more chances he took. In August of 1984, Chris, Gae, and the children were vacationing on Martha's Vineyard when Chris spotted a woman parasailing over an inlet and decided to give it a try. Having strapped himself into a harness that was being towed by a motorboat, he gave a signal and the boat took off. Chris quickly gained altitude, and when he was about ninety feet above the water he began waving at Gae and the kids with both hands. "He should have been holding on to the harness," an eyewitness said.

"Suddenly, the harness became loose," the witness said, "and he began to fall, frantically waving his arms in the air." (The harness, it turned out, was designed to carry no more than 180 pounds; Chris weighed over 200 pounds.) Reeve plunged nine stories into just four feet of water.

"He dropped like a rock," said artist Donald Widdis, who also witnessed the accident. Widdis raced down the beach to check on him, convinced that "no one could take a fall like that and not be severely injured or dead."

Incredibly, Chris, who had instinctively curled up in a ball as he fell, landed on his side. He lay in the water, moaning, until onlookers helped him ashore. Reeve suffered bruised ribs and was bleeding from the mouth, but within a few weeks he had fully recovered. "You're lucky," one of his rescuers told him, "you didn't break your neck."

Gae Exton would never forget that day. "I've never been so terrified," she said, "as when I saw him falling."

The following month, after being turned down for the lead in *Children of a Lesser God* (the role went to his friend William Hurt), Chris agreed to do his first made-for-television movie. He was to play Count Vronsky opposite Jacqueline Bisset in the CBS adaptation of Tolstoy's *Anna Karenina*. With a screenplay by *The Lion in Winter* author James Goldman and a cast that also included Academy Award–winner Paul Scofield, Chris looked forward to being part of what, for all intents and purposes, looked like a quality production. As for advisors who told him to wait for a vehicle of his own before making the jump to television: "I just thought: 'What a beautiful story. I'd like to be part of it.'"

Before filming began in Budapest, Chris decided to get some formal instruction in horseback riding from an instructor near his brother Ben's home in Martha's Vineyard. Once he arrived in Hungary, it quickly became apparent that Chris, who still took antihistamines to control his allergy to horses, needed all the professional help he could get. In one of *Anna Karenina*'s key scenes, Vronsky's horse is injured in a steeplechase and the count is forced to put him down with a single bullet. Chris had no experience jumping fences or hedges, but he did want to try to keep up with the other riders in the scene—all members of Hungary's national equestrian team—during the opening stretch on flat ground.

As it turned out, his horse tore away from the pack and out of range of the camera truck. After several takes, Chris was hooked. When he returned to the United States in late 1984, he decided to take up riding seriously. In addition to working with trainers in Bedford, New York, he often spent days at a time riding through the Green Mountains of Vermont. His mount for the Vermont rides, a temperamental mare named Hope, made a habit of throwing him off whenever the mood struck her. "She was definitely a tough cookie," he later said. "But she kept you on your toes."

Another of Chris's many close calls occurred on the set of his next film, one that Chris hoped would finally help him emerge from the long shadow of Superman. In the gritty *Street Smart,* Chris portrayed an ambitious young reporter whose manufactured stories land him in a dangerous spot between the police and a homicidal pimp (played by big-screen newcomer Morgan Freeman). Driven to once again prove his versatility as an actor, Chris refused to be sidelined by something so minor as an emergency appendectomy. Just two days after surgery, he defied doctor's orders and returned to the set—to do a fight scene. "Don't forget," Chris cautioned Freeman jokingly, "what happened to Houdini."

Street Smart earned an Oscar nomination for Freeman, but Chris's performance was widely panned. He had no illusions about what the reaction to his next project would be: Offered $4 million to reprise the role, Chris donned his cape yet again, for *Superman IV*. It was a decision, he later conceded, "I lived to regret." "*Superman IV,*" he said, "was a catastrophe from start to finish. That failure was a huge blow to my career." His next film, a clumsy remake of *The Front Page* called *Switching Channels,* hammered the final nail in Chris's professional coffin—"the end of my nine-year career as an above-the-line movie star."

By late 1986, Chris's decade-long relationship with Gae Exton was over. They agreed that she and the children would continue to live in the London house Chris had purchased for them, while Chris returned to live in New York. As for the children, "If the love is not in question, they can survive separation," he later said. "When we get together, we fall right into place."

For now, he and Gae were keeping the split out of the press. But later, Chris would insist "there was never an incident, never an act of cruelty or a betrayal between Gae and me. It was just a growing awareness that we were the wrong people for each other."

Reeve and Exton would, for the sake of the kids as much as anything else, remain friends. That did not, however, keep Chris from sinking into a deep depression. "I knew I would always be a part of their lives," he said, "but by separating, we were just acting out what I'd seen in my family over and over again. It was painful."

From the depths of his depression over the breakup, Reeve mulled his options. For the time being, he would retreat once more to the place where he felt safest: peaceful, bucolic, nurturing Williamstown. It was there that, in early 1987, he threw himself into renovating a cedar-sided contemporary house he bought just outside of town on Treadwell Hollow Road, for $260,000.

Situated on thirty-six hilltop acres with sweeping views of the Berkshires, the house boasted five bedrooms and seven bathrooms as well as a garage/barn big enough to accommodate Chris's glider. He placed a king-sized bed smack in the middle of the octagonal master bedroom, so that when he woke up there would be a dazzling vista in every direction.

By the summer of 1987, Chris was getting tired of waking up alone in that giant bed with the wraparound view. But before he could do anything about that, his half brothers Kevin and Jeff showed up to keep him company. They were joined at the end of July by Matthew and Alexandra, on vacation from school in London. As he attacked his role in the Williamstown production of *The Rover* with his customary laserlike intensity ("No one took his craft more seriously than Chris—*no one,*" said fellow cast member Edward Herrmann), Chris seemed genuinely content. "I'm at a place right now," he told one of his fellow actors, "where I'm feeling optimistic about things. Maybe I just don't need to be in a serious relationship to be happy."

Enter Dana. After that first meeting at the 1896 House cabaret show and the hour-long conversation at The Zoo that followed, Chris could not get her out of his mind. For the next ten days, he courted Dana in a manner that could have been straight out of the script for *Somewhere in Time.*

There was yet another random encounter—this time on a Williamstown street—during which the two were once again lost in conversation. The next day while biking near his home, Chris suddenly decided to stop and pick wildflowers for Dana along the side of the road. He gathered them up in a bunch, rushed back to the theater where Dana was rehearsing one of her cabaret numbers, and then just as suddenly got cold feet. Instead, he asked a coed to go inside and deliver the flowers to

Dana for him. The young woman was obviously delighted to act as a go-between.

Dana had just finished her number when the girl walked in from the wings and handed them to her. "Christopher Reeve asked me to give these to you," she said.

Dana's eyes widened with surprise and her hand went to her mouth. "You've got to be kidding," she said, then without missing a beat asked when and where he gave them to her.

"About two minutes ago," the coed answered.

Dana rushed outside to thank him, but Chris was gone. Embarrassed by his impulsive gesture—and, incredibly, fearing rejection—Chris had pedaled off "feeling stupid. It was all so corny, and for whatever reason, it occurred to me that maybe she would think I was a jerk."

If anything, Dana was both flattered and beguiled by this movie star who seemed so unsure of himself. Yet she was also more than a little suspicious. "It seemed a little fishy," she said, "that he could be quite so charming and obviously very shy. I kind of wondered what he was up to."

Her suspicions seemed confirmed when, after one cabaret performance, he asked if she'd like to drive over to Margaret Lindley Pond for a moonlight dip. "Oh, God," she thought, "here comes the old let's-get-naked-and-go-for-a-swim routine."

Before she could answer, Chris added, "I'll drive over to your place and you can pick up your bathing suit."

For Dana, who was both relieved and delighted, it was a defining moment in their relationship. "I thought," she later recalled, "that that was so sweet." As promised, Chris drove Dana back to the dorm where she was staying to pick up her swimsuit—which she put on under her clothes—and the two headed out to the pond. That night, they swam and engaged in a little chaste horse-play, splashing each other mercilessly. Then, in another scene straight out of old Hollywood, Chris pulled Dana toward him in the water, and they shared their first kiss.

Still, Dana wanted to take things slow. "I thought I would look at this as 'What I Did Last Summer,'" she said. "I didn't expect to really fall in love." Chris was equally wary. "I really wanted to make sure I was not getting into a relationship on the rebound," he admitted. "It was a case of what happens to you when you're not looking. Happiness sneaks up."

Caution aside, the romance quickly blossomed. There were dinners in town, picnics, and long drives along the narrow two-lane roads that snaked through the Massachusetts countryside. One of the things that most appealed to Dana was the fact that this major movie star tooled around in a black pickup with roll-down windows and an AM radio. "This guy is *cool*," Dana thought. Later, she recalled how they would "do all these things that were so down-to-earth. Which is what I'm like and what I like about people. I realized he wasn't just this movie star. I found that he was very much like me."

Soon they were parking in the middle of fields and, in Chris's words, "making out like teenagers." It was during one of these sessions, when the truck was parked on a treeless hilltop with only a few cows in view, that they consummated the affair.

Such privacy was not always attainable. On occasion, Chris would take Dana back to her dorm after the cabaret show and park outside—right next to a giant green refuse container heaped with festival garbage. While they necked in the distinctive black pickup, other actors would pass by and casually remark that Chris and Dana were inside steaming up the windows. "They were right on the verge," joked a theater apprentice who worked with Chris, "of becoming a tourist attraction."

"We knew something was going on between Chris and Dana," said Jennifer Van Dyke, who was performing alongside Chris in *The Rover*. "But there were lots of summer romances going on at the time. Compared to some other people, they were pretty discreet about it."

Chris's friend Edward Herrmann at first saw Dana as "another one of the beautiful, talented young fillies who came up to Williamstown every summer. She was leggy and gorgeous and we were all jealous as hell. But I thought it was just another pleasant Williamstown summer fling." Soon he and the rest of the Williamstown Festival community came to the realization that "they had really fallen for each other. This was the real deal."

Before they could read about it in the gossip columns, Dana decided to share the news of her celebrity romance with a few of her closest friends. One of the first people she called was her longtime pal Michael Manganiello.

"I've met somebody," she said, hesitating.

"What?" Manganiello said.

"Well, he's kind of famous."

"So who is it?" Manganiello asked.

"Well, I'm kind of dating Christopher Reeve."

Manganiello paused for a moment. "You're dating Superman?" he asked.

Kidding aside, Chris and Dana had legitimate reasons for trying to keep their romance under wraps. To begin with, Chris and

Gae had not yet gone public with their split. Even more important, Matthew and Alexandra were staying with Chris at the
Williamstown house, and he did not want to confuse or upset his
young children by showing up with a woman other than their
mother.

It would be nearly two months before Chris brought Dana
home for dinner with the kids. If he had any worries about how
they would react to this new woman in Dad's life, they quickly
vanished. Dana's natural, easygoing manner, her boundless energy,
and her window-rattling laugh made her an instant hit with
Matthew and Alexandra. Soon Dana was joining them for spirited
miniature golf tournaments, marathon bike rides, and some good-
natured roughhousing on the front lawn.

The one thing Dana did not do was stay over. Chris was still
not sure what the kids would think if they saw Dad sharing a bed
with Dana. Gae showed up in late August to bring three-year-old
Alexandra back to London, leaving Matthew, seven, to spend a
little more time with his father.

At this stage, Dana was still reluctant to risk alienating Chris's
children. By the time her parents came to see her perform at
Williamstown, she was still not staying overnight at the Reeve
house. Over dinner at a local restaurant, Chris told the Morosinis
that he "enjoyed dating" their daughter. "I mean, she's so much
fun, so wonderful. We have a great time together . . ."

Without missing a beat, Chris then launched into a description
of the house he was still renovating. "The master bedroom is huge
and has an octagonal shape with windows facing in every direction," Chris told them, scarcely trying to conceal his enthusiasm.
"There's a spiral staircase leading up to it, and this big king-size

California bed right in the middle of the room that is *so* comfortable."

Charles Morosini studied Chris's face for a moment, and cocked his head quizzically. Before he could ask Chris if he was seriously talking to him about his and Dana's sleeping habits, Dana hastily changed the subject.

In fact, Chris was still concerned about Matthew walking in and finding his dad beneath the sheets with Dana. So he waited until they went sailing off the coast of Maine with Uncle Kevin aboard Chris's forty-foot yacht, *Chandelle*. The first morning at sea, Matthew, who slept in the main cabin, walked to the bow to find Chris and Dana sharing the same bed. Dana, unfazed, pulled back the covers and invited Matthew to snuggle. As soon he settled in, Dana ambushed him with tickles. In retaliation, Matthew clobbered her with a pillow, and soon there was chaos in the forward part of the cabin. "We laughed *so* hard," Dana told a friend, "but I told them we had to stop before somebody fell overboard."

It was the breakthrough Chris had been hoping for. Matthew's easy acceptance of Dana opened the way for an even more relaxed and open relationship. Now, when Dana sang during the cabaret show at Williamstown, Chris joined her onstage for a duet or two. Perched on stools and clutching microphones, Dana and Chris were, said one regular audience member, "obviously besotted with each other." Their repertoire nearly always included two standards: the Gershwins' "Let's Call the Whole Thing Off" and Cole Porter's "It's De-Lovely," the tune they would come to think of as "our song."

Now that Chris publicly acknowledged his break from Gae Exton, the press was quick to paint Dana as the scheming Other

Woman. Apparently relying on reports that Dana had spent a considerable amount of time with Matthew and Alexandra, one tabloid story stated that she had been hired to care for them. "SUPERMAN," the headline blared, "DUMPS HIS KIDS' MOM FOR BABYSITTER."

That fall, they continued their affair in New York. While Chris was ensconced in his duplex co-op on West Seventy-eighth Street near the American Museum of Natural History, Dana shared a modest apartment with her sister. It was not long before Dana was spending nearly all her time at Chris's apartment.

They quickly discovered that there were some differences in their approach to housekeeping. "My side of the bed is neat," observed Chris, whose passion for order would soon get on Dana's nerves. "Hers looks like a yard sale. Sometimes it gets to me and I say, 'Clutter alert.'"

He may have been a household name, but Chris, like Dana, was now forced to audition for every role. With one exception. Asked to join a TV ad campaign for Maidenform Bra that included the likes of Pierce Brosnan, Omar Sharif, and Michael York, Superman agreed—and gratefully pocketed the $300,000 fee.

Chris and Dana hied away to Williamstown once more, determined to enjoy a quiet Thanksgiving holiday at their idyllic New England retreat. The last thing they had on their minds was political turmoil in South America. But when exiled Chilean writer Ariel Dorfman phoned him in Williamstown and requested his help, Chris was eager to hear what he had to say.

Ever since General Augusto Pinochet seized power in Chile in 1973, anyone who dared speak out against his regime feared imprisonment, torture, or worse; by the fall of 1987, thousands of Chileans had been executed, assassinated—or simply disappeared. Now Pinochet had ordered seventy-seven actors in the capital city of Santiago to leave the country by November 30 or face execution.

The seventy-seven condemned actors were standing their ground, and now an international group of actors was being assembled by Amnesty International to stand beside them as the deadline approached. Dorfman asked Chris if he was willing to be the group's sole U.S. member. Chris sat on the governing council of Actors' Equity, but more important, as Superman he was recognized the world over as a symbol of truth, justice, and democracy.

The mission was not without its risks. Pinochet's henchmen had shown no compunction about assassinating foes of the regime. Chris asked Dana what she thought.

"You really don't have any choice, Chris," she said without hesitating. "Do it."

During his week-long visit to Santiago, Chris was scheduled to speak at a rally in support of the actors threatened with execution. More than seven thousand people packed Santiago's Santa Laura Stadium, but when police turned fire hoses on the crowd, the rally moved to an abandoned parking garage in another part of the city. Pinochet's forces encircled the building, tear-gassing the overflow crowd and awaiting orders to open fire. Those orders never came.

Instead, inside the garage there were poetry readings and telegrams from abroad proclaiming solidarity with the actors. The high point came when Chris stood up to declare support among U.S. citizens for Chile's embattled artistic community. When he finished with the promise to return to the United States and tell his countrymen what "brave and beautiful people you are," the crowd erupted in cheers. "Superman! Superman!" they chanted.

The next day, several South American newspapers carried stories pitting Chris against one of the region's most feared strongmen. "SUPERMAN VS. PINOCHET" screamed one headline, while another read "SUPERMAN TO THE RESCUE!" Several underground newspapers ran editorial cartoons showing Chris in full Superman garb, taking on a bloated, bemedaled, jackbooted Pinochet.

In the end, the dreaded November 30 deadline passed without any of the threatened executions taking place. Less than five months later, Pinochet would bow to pressure and resign the presidency. Dorfman, among others, would give Reeve some of the credit for starting the ball rolling. "To many, Christopher Reeve and Superman are inseparable," he said. "To think that Superman is on your side, even on a subconscious level, is a powerful thing. Chris gave the people of Chile hope at a time when they desperately needed it, and for that we shall always be grateful to him."

Chris insisted this was "not Superman to the rescue . . . If you know me as Superman, fine. But we have to remember that Superman is light entertainment. This was real life."

Dana "could not have been prouder of Chris" when he returned to Williamstown. "Chris is just a profoundly passionate, committed guy," she said. "He's the complete opposite of superficial, but some people don't take him seriously because he is just so damned good-looking. If they only knew, he's even better on the *inside*."

That Christmas of 1987, Exton dropped both Matthew and Alexandra off with Chris to spend the holidays in Williamstown.

Again, Chris worried about how Alexandra, who like Matthew sounded very British despite their dual citizenship, was going to react to seeing Daddy in bed with someone other than Mummy.

Reeve's fears proved unfounded. In addition to his posh accent and blond hair, "Al" shared her brother's mischievous streak. Every morning at dawn, they tiptoed in, then gleefully leapt on the bed. For the next half hour, "it was nothing but tickles and giggles," Reeve said. "Dana seemed to enjoy it as much as they did."

Once they were back in New York, both Chris and Dana once again had to scramble for work. That January of 1988, Chris flew to Los Angeles to star on stage as the womanizing John Buchanan in Tennessee Williams's southern Gothic psychodrama *Summer and Smoke.*

After a few weeks, Dana called up one of Chris's pals with her plan to pay him a surprise visit. "I thought it would be fun to fly out there," she said. "Think of the expression on his face when I just show up."

All too familiar with Chris's tendency to stray, the friend was less than enthusiastic about Dana's plan. "Umm, gee . . . ," he said, screwing up his face and shaking his head, "I don't think that's a good idea. Don't surprise him. Surprises aren't good."

"Why not?" It took a few seconds for Dana to get the not-so-subtle message. "Oh. Well," she said with a shrug, "if I'm going to go out there and find him with someone else, it might as well be now."

When she called the theater and checked with the manager's office, she was told that Chris was throwing a party for the entire cast and crew at a popular Thai restaurant called Tommy Tang's. Dana drove up alone in a cab and found her way to the private room where Chris's *Summer and Smoke* party was being held. Chris was easy to spot in any room—he towered over nearly everyone—and when she saw him, drink in hand, completely engrossed in conversation with someone she couldn't see at the far end of the room, her heart sank for an instant. She took a deep breath and made her way through the crowd toward Chris. She found him engaged in a heartfelt conversation with a burly electrician.

"Dana!" Chris yelled, wrapping her up in his arms and lifting her off the floor.

"So, I expected to find you with a gorgeous blonde," she half-joked.

"Hey," Chris shot back, motioning to the surfer-blond electrician, "do you want to hurt Jim's feelings?"

They had been together for a solid six months, and neither was certain that their relationship could withstand a lengthy separation. Now that they had their answer, the relief in their voices and on their faces was unmistakable.

"I missed you," Chris said as he plucked two glasses of champagne off a passing silver tray.

"I missed you too," Dana answered, holding her glass up to toast the moment.

They stood in the same spot and talked for more than an hour, and as on the night they first met, everything and everyone else just seemed to vanish.

"Dana is my life force."

—*Chris*

"I didn't fall in love with Superman.
I fell in love with a super man."

—*Dana*

3

It had been an idyllic few months in L.A. during the limited run of *Summer and Smoke,* with Dana and Chris sharing his rented stucco-walled bungalow off Laurel Canyon Boulevard, on winding Tiana Road. Chris had assayed the role of the boozing John Buchanan twice before, but now he worried that maybe his portrayal had grown stale. He asked Dana to stay and help him find new ways to approach the part.

Once again putting her own career on hold, Dana sat in the audience night after night, taking notes and later offering suggestions. "She made me see things in the part of Johnny I'd never seen before," he said. "It's one of the stage performances I'm proudest of, and I give a lot of the credit to Dana."

That spring, Chris headed for Yugoslavia to shoot the two-part NBC miniseries *The Great Escape II.* In the sequel to the classic 1963 film starring Steve McQueen and James Garner, Chris was cast as Major John Dodge, a German POW who actually fought in both world wars, swam the English Channel, and climbed the Matterhorn. As always, Chris thoroughly researched the part, and discovered that he and the adventurous Major Dodge bore an uncanny resemblance to each other.

Shortly after filming began, Dana joined Chris on location. It was their first trip abroad together, and as they explored the ancient villages and wild terrain along the border between Slovenia and Croatia, the American lovers found themselves, in Dana's words, "swept away by the beauty and romance of it all. It was very exciting."

Much of the excitement apparently stemmed from the manner in which they were touring the Yugoslav countryside. While they had done a little riding the previous summer in Williamstown, this trip abroad marked the first time that Chris and Dana set out to spend entire days on horseback. Several times a week, they would ride up to Mokrice, a turreted, six-hundred-year-old castle-turned-hotel, for an afternoon tryst before returning to the set.

From the outset, it was clear that Dana was far the superior horsewoman. As with everything he did in life, Chris took an all-out approach to the sport, often taking off without warning across an open field or, in one or two instances, jumping a low hedge or a narrow brook. Dana could easily keep up, but as a trained equestrienne she erred on the side of caution. "Whoa, Chris," she called out to him as he raced ahead, "what's the rush? We don't have to kill ourselves."

It was a concern that had been shared by at least one of Chris's teachers. Kristen Hyduchak was first approached by Chris in 1989 when he began training at the Westchester County stable where she worked. Over the next two years, she observed him frequently—often several times a week—and was not happy with what she saw.

Almost from the beginning, Chris was trying to jump—this despite the fact that, according to Hyduchak, he was "still having trouble with the basics—walk, trot, canter. He used to scream my name to help him all the time," she continued. "'Kristen,' he would yell, 'I can't get my horse to trot.' I'd help him get it right. The next day, he'd have the same problem."

Yet what bothered Hyduchak most from the start was the way Chris sat in the saddle. He had a tendency, she noted, to shift his weight forward as he rode. "There is always a risk that way," she said, "of going over the horse's head."

Yet Dana was impressed with how Chris, who had far more experience at the helm of a yacht than he did astride a stallion, carried himself in the saddle. For a large man who sometimes looked, she said, "as if his feet were going to drag on the ground," Chris exuded "complete confidence and control up there."

Moreover, his lifelong allergy to horses required Chris to down sizable quantities of antihistamines—and even then his eyes periodically puffed up and watered. "I was miserable some of the time," he conceded, "but I tried not to let Dana see that."

Chris's performance as a horseman was indeed calculated in part to impress the woman he loved. "She is a wonderful rider— a real pro," he allowed. "I mean, she's been doing this since she was six! I wanted her to know that I wasn't a total tenderfoot when it came to horses—that I could keep up."

Conversely, Dana pushed aside her natural inclination toward seasickness and embraced Chris's love of sailing. Over the years,

they would cruise up and down the Eastern Seaboard, exploring the coastline from Nova Scotia down to the Chesapeake.
More than once, she came up from belowdecks looking, Chris
said, "a little green around the gills." But she never whined, and
over time proved that nothing—not even a raging storm or the
imminent threat of being dashed against a rock in rough seas—
could rattle her.

On one excursion north to Nova Scotia, the *Chandelle* encountered a fog bank and began to drift dangerously close to the
rocky shore. While Chris and his half brother Kevin sweated out
the arrival of the Canadian Coast Guard, Dana seemed unper-
turbed. After a Coast Guard cutter showed up in the nick of time
to tow the *Chandelle* and its passengers to safety, Dana thanked
the cutter's crew by whipping up some breakfast and serving it
to them on deck.

These shared passions only served to draw Chris and Dana
closer together. "One of the things that's so great about Dana,"
he gushed to one writer when they returned to the United
States, "is we sail together, we dive together, we ride together.
She plays a good game of tennis. She's a great dancer. She laughs
all the time. She thinks life is to be enjoyed. So I've got a great
partner."

Now when they returned to Williamstown for the summer,
they both felt they were returning to their house. "Gae really had
had nothing to do with the Williamstown house," Chris explained,
"but Dana's influence was everywhere. We felt like a real couple."

While his personal life was coming together, Chris found he was
persona non grata as far as major Hollywood producers were concerned. He stormed out of an audition for *Pretty Woman* when it

became clear that the director Garry Marshall was not seriously considering him for the lead role (it went to Richard Gere). When it came time to bring Tom Wolfe's blockbuster novel *The Bonfire of the Vanities* to the screen, Chris met with the producers and made an impassioned plea as to why he was perfect for the part.

"I know this guy. I *am* this guy," he said of the book's Ivy League–educated Park Avenue protagonist. "There is no part of him that I don't understand, and there is no part of him that I can't play."

The producers agreed. "You would be absolutely perfect," one said. "I think you'd be great casting for the role, and there's no way we're giving you this part."

No one had to explain why. "What was not being said," Chris later explained, "and I mean the 'filling in the blanks' said, was 'I'm not going with somebody who hasn't had a hit in two years.'"

Chris began taking jobs he wouldn't even have considered just a few years earlier. He was forced to stand idly by as *Saturday Night Live*'s Dana Carvey hosted *Superman's Fiftieth Anniversary: A Celebration of the Man of Steel* on CBS, but Chris jumped at the chance to host another prime-time TV special: *The World's Greatest Stunts: A Tribute to Hollywood Stuntmen*.

No one who knew the thrill-seeking Chris was surprised when he agreed to do the stuntman special. It quickly became clear that, in making the special, he was eager to take some chances of his own. At one point during the shooting, Chris stood on the tarmac as a small plane zoomed out of the sky and headed straight for him.

"It was Chris's idea to end the special that way," the plane's pilot, Jim Petri, recalled. "I could hardly believe what he was asking." When it came time to shoot the scene, Petri went on, "I headed right for him at about eighty miles an hour. He dropped to his knees just before one wing passed over him and I breathed a sigh of relief."

Incredibly, Chris drew himself up and asked to shoot the stunt again. The screams of crew members on the ground, terrified as they watched the plane pass just inches over Chris's head, were clearly audible on the tape. He felt they were too distracting.

As always, Dana was impressed by Chris's bravado. But she was also concerned that he would someday push the envelope too far. "The show was a tribute to Hollywood stuntmen," she cracked, "not a tribute to dead actors trying to do their own stunts."

As horrifying as Chris's stunt special was, it was not nearly as shocking as the news he and Dana received from his business manager in 1989. Britain's Inland Revenue Service was claiming that, since all four of his *Superman* films were shot largely in England, he owed $1 million in back taxes to the UK.

To pay off this whopping tax debt—not to mention support a lifestyle that included a New York apartment, a country house, a seven-passenger Cheyenne II turboprop he referred to as "Mike," a glider, and a yacht—Chris took on even more television work. In the span of a few months, he hosted an environmental documentary titled *Our Common Future, Night of 100 Stars III,* the *16th Annual People's Choice Awards, The Earthday Party,* and the highly rated *Valvoline National Driving Test,* which also featured the diverse likes of Betty White, Paul Newman, and Walter Cronkite.

There would still be challenging roles onstage—in Joseph Papp's production of *The Winter's Tale* at New York's Public Theater, in a national tour of A. R. Gurney's *Love Letters* playing opposite Julie Hagerty, and of course in numerous productions at Williamstown. But increasingly, it was the acting he did on the small screen—particularly in made-for-TV movies—that paid the bills.

Starting with *The Rose and the Jackal* on Ted Turner's TNT network—a Civil War–era drama in which a bearded Reeve portrayed Secret Service founder Allan Pinkerton—Chris starred in a Lifetime network thriller called *Death Dreams* and the CBS movie of the week *Bump in the Night,* followed by Disney's *Road to Avonlea,* PBS's *The Road from Runnymeade,* HBO's *Tales from the Crypt,* and the USA Network's *Mortal Sins*—all in the span of twenty months.

Despite his prolific output on television, Chris was no longer being asked to spend months at a time on a movie set. That meant he had more time to devote to the causes he felt passionately about. A committed environmentalist, he narrated a documentary on the *Exxon Valdez* oil spill, spearheaded a campaign to block a coal-fired electric plant in upstate New York, urged legislators in Albany to enact a law that allowed private citizens to sue polluters, and went to Washington to urge passage of the federal Clean Air Act.

One of Chris's pet crusades ended up pitting him against real estate mogul Donald Trump. Chris had joined others in protesting The Donald's plans to build a huge development bearing his name on Manhattan's West Side. But when the two men met face-to-face at Trump's offices on Fifth Avenue, they quickly discovered they could work together to make Trump City more palatable to West Siders. "It was," Trump later said, "the start of a beautiful friendship."

The list of Chris's humanitarian works—causes in which
Dana became no less involved—ranged from Save the Children
and ChildHope to the National Jewish Hospital for Asthma Research, the American Heart and Lung Association, Amnesty International, and MADD (Mothers Against Drunk Driving). A
turning point came when Reeve, outraged by attempts to cut
back funding for the National Endowment for the Arts, teamed
up with actors Ron Silver, Blair Brown, Stephen Collins, and Bedford neighbor Susan Sarandon to form a group called the Creative Coalition. In addition to coming to the defense of the
embattled National Endowment for the Arts, the Creative Coalition took on such issues as homelessness, campaign finance reform, health care, and the environment. "Chris was incredibly
persuasive," said actor William Baldwin, who later served as the
Coalition's president. "We were all passionate and well informed
on the issues, but nobody was more effective than Chris at winning people over. He was so calm, so measured, and so self-
assured—he was a down-to-earth guy, but he also always brought
a certain dignity to the proceedings."

Not surprisingly, Chris soon drew the attention of Democratic Party officials. "It was hard to imagine a more attractive and
articulate candidate than Christopher Reeve," said Al Gore, who
urged Chris to run for office. "I mean, come on, he's Superman!"
On the sudden death in 1991 of Massachusetts Republican Sil-
vio Conte, who represented the Williamstown area in Congress,
several Democratic party leaders urged Chris to run for the seat.
"What?" he replied, "and lose my influence in Washington?"
Reeve was dead serious. As a movie star recognized by millions
as the personification of truth, justice, and the American way,

Chris commanded far more attention than any one congressman
or senator.

For all of his accomplishments, the fact remained that Chris
was relying more heavily than ever on Dana—and not merely for
emotional support. Every year, Matthew and Alexandra were sent
to live with their father. But in truth, it was Dana who dropped
everything to care for them—a burden she gladly undertook.
"They were so darling and fantastic," she recalled, "that when it
was time for them to visit, I'd literally drop everything. I wouldn't
take auditions. I wouldn't do jobs. Family, even before it was my
official family, was always my priority."

Gae Exton, too, had always kept family as her first priority. But
Gae also had her own life, her own career apart from Chris; she
could stand on her own financially and emotionally. The things
that, aside from her beauty, initially appealed to Chris most about
Gae—this abiding sense of independence, her British reserve, and
the fact that she was not particularly interested in show business
or the celebrities it spawned—were what actually may have stood
in the way of a permanent commitment.

In Dana, Chris had found someone who understood his
world completely because she was a part of it. She was also open
and warm and funny—and clearly willing to make sacrifices if
that's what it took to make the man she loved happy.

Indeed, it was Dana's desire to partake fully in Chris's life that
set her apart from anyone he had ever known. She shared his love
of acting without ever wanting to compete with him (Chris's
previous affairs with actresses were "doomed by our egos," he
once cracked). She cherished his children. She took up his favorite
causes, standing beside him at meetings and rallies, working dili-

gently behind the scenes to help him polish his speeches. She fell in love with the place he now called home, Williamstown, and, like Chris, could hardly wait to return there every summer and on the holidays.

Then there was the outdoor life that made Chris the man he was—the skiing, the tennis, the biking, the flying, the riding, and, perhaps most important, the sailing. Dana had become so enamored of the sport, in fact, that when Chris decided he wanted to sell the *Chandelle* in late 1989 and build a bigger, faster boat of his own, she urged him to do it.

Her reasons were perhaps not altogether unselfish. "Chris had a lot of memories tied up with that boat that didn't include Dana," said a friend. "Like any woman, she wanted to start fresh and have them make memories of their own as a couple. I'm sure Chris was aware of that, and he was happy to please her."

They contracted to have the Cambria 46 custom-built in Portsmouth, Rhode Island—an expensive venture that Chris offset in part by selling one of his planes for $300,000. For weeks before the keel was laid, Dana and Chris pored over the design to determine every aspect of the boat, from the shape of the hull and the location of the galley to the brass fixtures on deck. They quickly agreed on a name: *Sea Angel.*

On the day their new yacht was christened, Dana handed Chris an album chronicling the birth of *Sea Angel.* It was a gesture that nearly brought him to tears, and left him more convinced than ever that Dana was the one. "I was feeling more and more," he later said, "that we were meant to be together."

Dana agreed. The boat wasn't the only thing she thought to replace in their lives. Dana had never really felt completely comfortable in the Upper West Side duplex. This was where Chris, Gae, and their children had lived for years as a family; the cherry trees they planted on their roof garden were a constant reminder to Dana of the life Chris had led before they met. "The apartment is beautiful, and I love the neighborhood," Dana confided to a friend. "But I still sort of feel like a guest there."

Dana told Chris that it was time they picked up and moved to another Manhattan neighborhood where they could make memories of their own. Besides, at twenty-nine Dana felt the Upper West Side was a little too stodgy for her taste; she wanted to relocate to a trendier neighborhood farther downtown. Tribeca, perhaps, or maybe Chelsea.

Chris had other ideas. Despite his devotion to Dana, his feelings about the institution of marriage remained unchanged. And by setting up a new household, it seemed to Chris as if they were taking a major step toward the altar.

Dana "wasn't pressing Chris about marriage at all," one of his closest friends recalled. "But she did want them to have a committed relationship, a real future as a couple. Setting up a place of their own, far from the ghosts of Chris's past, was part of that."

In the meantime, Dana was seriously considering a move to California. In the spring of 1990, she played the Julia Roberts part in a television pilot based on the blockbuster film *Steel Magnolias*. The series was never produced, but Dana wondered if she was losing out on important opportunities by not being in Los Angeles.

Worried that she might pull up stakes and leave, Chris finally relented in the fall of 1990 and sold his beloved Upper West Side duplex for $1 million. They settled on an eight-room penthouse on East Twenty-second Street in New York's up-and-coming Flatiron District. The apartment boasted brick walls, high ceilings, and a glassed-in atrium with dazzling midtown views.

Dana reveled in their new digs, eschewing the Gae Exton–inspired English shabby-chic look of the West Seventy-eighth Street apartment in favor of oversized white cotton sofas and chairs, jewel-toned carpets, and glass-topped tables heaped with books and flowers. Chris was a willing accomplice in Dana's desire to make the Flatiron District their new neighborhood. The dined at nearby Union Square Cafe and City Crab, prowled stores like ABC Carpet and Fish's Eddy for treasures, and on weekends stocked up on fresh produce at the outdoor Greenmarket in Union Square.

"You get the feeling of being sort of a pioneer down here, that you're more on the cutting edge," Dana observed, noting that the downtown New York scene provided a "nice contrast" to their permanent residence in bucolic Williamstown. "This area of the city is grittier, noisier, younger, more alive. That's what I love about it."

If Dana thought that by starting fresh Chris would suddenly realize they had a future together as a couple, she was sadly mistaken. Whenever she hinted at the possibility of a long-term commitment, he became more intransigent than ever. Chris still told anyone who would listen that he had no intention of following previous generations of Reeves down the primrose path to matrimony and, inevitably, bitter divorce.

"What about my parents?" Dana asked. "They've been married forever and they're still in love."

"Your mom and dad," he replied with a shrug, "are the exception that proves the rule."

Exasperated, Dana made it clear that she definitely saw marriage in her future, even if he did not see it in his. "I love you, Chris," she told him. "But I want a family, too. I want what my parents have . . ."

Even if he had wanted to change, Chris felt powerless to overcome his fear of marriage. While Dana fumed, Chris left for Vancouver in the summer of 1991 to make his first feature film in four years. In *Morning Glory,* he was cast as an ex-con who becomes involved with a recently widowed young mother (Deborah Raffin) in Depression-era Texas.

Before he left New York, Chris made Dana promise that she would join him in British Columbia midway through the shoot. He made plans to charter a boat and sail from Vancouver to Galiano Island, the most ruggedly beautiful of British Columbia's Gulf Islands. There, they would stay in a suite at the island's only oceanfront resort, the Galiano Inn.

For the next two months, Dana and Chris burned up the phone lines between Vancouver and New York. Why was he so intractable on the subject of marriage? What was he really afraid of? "If you really love someone," she said point-blank, "then to me that means you commit to the relationship—or you lose that person. Is that what you want, Chris?"

"No, of course not," he replied. But neither was he willing— or able—to overcome his profound feelings of dread when it came to the subject of marriage. He had been so scarred by the cycle of divorce, remarriage, and divorce that had characterized his childhood that Chris could offer no solutions. They had reached a stalemate.

Conceding defeat, Dana finally called it quits. "It's over, Chris," she told him during one of their emotional late-night phone calls. "There is no future for us. There is just no point to going on like this if you can't even . . . It's . . . it's just over."

Chris pleaded with her to reconsider, but she held firm. Dana did, however, reluctantly agree to go ahead with their original plans to sail to Galiano Island—one of the most breathtaking spots in the Pacific Northwest—so long as things between them remained strictly platonic.

No sooner did she step onto the pier at Galiano Island than Dana realized her resolve to end their relationship would be put to the test. There were moonlight strolls along the beach, a bike ride through the island's lush Pacific Coast forest, candlelit dinners, and drinks by the fireside. If Dana and Chris thought there was any way they could restrain themselves from making love, it was answered their first night on the island: They could not.

In what Chris would later describe as "the most agonizingly bittersweet time," they both confronted the fact that, in Dana's words, "we couldn't live without each other. But there were going to have to be some changes made." At long last, Chris agreed to Dana's oft-repeated plea that he seek help from a therapist in dealing with his fear of commitment.

After months of therapy, thirty-nine-year-old Chris would finally admit that, beyond the legacy of his parents' dismal marital track record, he had his own ulterior motives for avoiding matrimony. "I was in a cycle of trying to maintain a relationship," he conceded, "but secretly looking for the ultimate babe."

Conversely, Chris also knew that he "risked everything" if he failed to deal with his own deeply rooted anxieties. "It came down to one thing," he later explained. "Was I going to be a damn fool and let this incredible woman walk out of my life?"

There would soon be an added incentive for Chris to finally, in Dana's words, "get a grip" on what was holding him back in the relationship. A few weeks after returning from their idyllic days on Galiano Island, Dana began feeling exhausted. "It was unusual for Dana," Chris recalled. "She's one of the few people in the world I have a hard time keeping up with—and that's saying something."

Stumped as to the cause of this nagging fatigue, Dana asked her older sister, Deborah, who was studying medicine at Boston University, if she had any theories. Deborah, who was pregnant, recognized the symptoms immediately. Dana, however, had already rejected the possibility that she could be pregnant; she and Chris had always been scrupulous when it came to birth control. "Nope," Dana concluded. "That couldn't be it. Maybe the flu?"

Deborah's diagnosis was right on the mark. A sonogram taken in December showed that Dana was already four months pregnant with a baby boy. Since the sonogram was taken at a doctor's office in New York's Murray Hill neighborhood, she and Chris referred to their future son as "Murray."

Dana, unprepared for this sudden turn of events, went ahead with plans to go to L.A. for a series of TV and film auditions. Concealing her swelling belly beneath roomy jackets and billowy blouses, she spent a week going from tryout to tryout before finally coming home.

"It was my way of sort of saying I wasn't going to let this baby get in my way," Dana recalled. "Then I thought, *Yes, I am going to let this baby get in my way!*"

A few days before Christmas 1991, with the lights of midtown Manhattan twinkling in the distance, Dana and Chris sat down to a romantic candlelit dinner. They had scarcely begun when their eyes locked and they both said simultaneously, "Let's get married!"

"Saying that," he later recalled, "was the sexiest thing." Indeed, no sooner had the words left their lips than they both put down their forks and headed straight for the bedroom. "I have never been happier, never," he said years later. "It was a moment whose time had come. . . . It was," Chris added, "extremely erotic."

In her more plainspoken way, Dana agreed. "Yep," she conceded, "it was a real turn-on."

So much so that Chris found himself waltzing around the Williamstown house and the apartment singing, "We're getting married!" Dana was more subdued, although she was more than willing to joke about what was appropriate attire for a visibly pregnant bride. "I want it to be as flattering as possible," she told one reporter. "I guess I'll show off legs and make a bonus of the cleavage."

Chris had his own ideas: "Make sure the dress has a window in it," he insisted.

"Yes," she continued, "for the ring-bearer inside."

Photographer Robin Bowman, who had been assigned to shoot the happy couple for *People,* recalled they were "obviously very much in love and thrilled about the baby." But even in the middle of Manhattan, Chris was eager to do something daring for the camera. He suggested Bowman shoot him repairing a cracked pane in the atrium window, which required climbing outside on a narrow balcony.

Immersed in her subject, Bowman forgot where she was—until she looked down and saw the pavement several stories below. "I froze," she recalled.

"You look like you're in trouble," Chris said when he realized that the photographer was in an awkward position and unable to climb down.

"So there I was," Bowman said later, "being rescued by Superman." As for Dana: "She was warm and friendly. He was obviously used to being in control—he told me from the beginning what he would and wouldn't do, and where and how he wanted to be photographed. Dana went along, but he also treated her with great respect. It was obvious they had a real partnership."

For the time being, Dana had her hands full balancing morning sickness and a lead part in the off-Broadway production of Donald Margulies's play *Sight Unseen*. Chris, in turn, was busy promoting his latest film, Peter Bogdanovich's screen version of the hit Broadway comedy *Noises Off*. He was paid $100,000—less than he had been paid for any film since *Superman*. Despite some glowing reviews ("No farce lover should miss it," raved *Newsweek*) and a cast that included Carol Burnett and Michael Caine, the movie bombed.

No matter. On April 11, a drizzly Saturday, the bride and groom, Matthew and Alexandra, and about forty-five other guests gathered at Field Farm in South Williamstown for the wedding of Christopher Reeve and Dana Morosini. Wearing a scoop-neck satin maternity top, a single strand of pearls, and baby's breath in her upswept hair, Dana clutched a bouquet of lilies of the valley as she walked down the aisle.

The newlyweds both realized that it had taken some considerable effort to get to this point. "All of the garbage in our relationship," Dana said in her characteristically direct manner, "was worked out before we got married."

Before a minister who moonlighted as a white-water rafting guide, the couple exchanged vows they had written and simple gold bands. Although no one could have known what the future held, those in attendance were emotionally undone by what was said.

"We made it very clear," Dana later said, "that we wanted to be married for better or worse. The choice was made then . . . You make these vows like, I will be with you whether things are always as terrific as they are at this moment or if they are the worst you can possibly imagine. I will stand by you. If you lose all your hair. If you lose every employment opportunity. We are now one. We go through this life as one."

When they were finished, everyone—including the bride and groom—was sobbing. At one point the official wedding video began shaking because the cameraman, Chris's brother Ben, was crying.

As they left the church, they were pelted with rice. "God, I love being married, I love it," Chris kept repeating. "This is a good deal!" According to Dana, Chris made this declaration every day for their first year as husband and wife. "Why," he would say as Dana shook her head in wonder, "didn't we do this before?"

There was no honeymoon. With a baby on the horizon, she went back onstage to finish her run in *Sight Unseen* and he went back on the road to promote *Noises Off.* That May, Chris and Dana attended the premiere of the new Merchant Ivory film, *Howards End,* at Lincoln Center. Chris told his old friend from *The Bostonians,* James Ivory, that he would take any part in the team's next film. Ivory phoned the next day and asked Chris if he would be interested in a small but important part in their next film, *The Remains of the Day.*

Chris told Ivory he did not need to see the script first. His answer was an emphatic "Yes."

Two months after the wedding, on June 7, 1992, Dana gave birth at North Adams Regional Hospital near Williamstown. Little Murray was now William Elliot Reeve, named after Chris's great-great-grandfather and the community where Chris and Dana met, fell in love, and planted roots: Williamstown.

After just two years in their East Twenty-second Street apartment, Dana and Chris pulled up stakes and moved yet again—this time to a century-old farmhouse on seven acres they purchased for $980,000. The property was situated just fifty miles northeast of Manhattan, in the Westchester County town of Bedford, not far from Dana's parents. While Bedford had more than its share of secluded estates (Martha Stewart's cozy $16 million "farm-house" among them), the town retained a certain rustic charm.

Ostensibly, they were making the move because they did not want to raise their child in the middle of a noisy, congested city. But Chris had his own reasons for wanting to relocate: The move would give him more time to practice his riding skills. Even Dana had to admit that, next to his family and acting, riding had become the most important thing in Chris's life. "He rides every day, is completely involved," she said. "He practices, watches videos. He is absolutely obsessed."

Some of those videos were, in fact, taken by Dana. Determined to share in every aspect of Chris's life, she went to nearly all of his competitions, frequently videotaping his performance so he could learn from his mistakes.

This grand obsession aside, Chris never hesitated to leave his horses behind when a location shoot beckoned. Now, whenever he signed on to do a feature film or TV film, Chris's contract stipulated that he would be provided quarters large enough to accommodate himself, Dana, Will, Matthew, Alexandra, and the nanny. Will was a colicky one-month-old when the entire tribe picked up and headed for Vancouver to film Jack London's classic *The Sea Wolf.*

That fall, Dana and Will tagged along when Chris journeyed to England to film *The Remains of the Day.* In the film, which revolves around the stifled relationship between a butler (Anthony Hopkins) and a housekeeper (Emma Thompson), Reeve played a young American congressman trying to convince his aristocratic British hosts to wake up to the threat posed by the Nazis. There was plenty of time between takes for the tight little family unit to tour the picturesque villages, medieval castles, and stately homes for which England's West Country was famous. In a year that produced *Schindler's List* and *The Piano, The Remains of the Day* would go on to earn eight Academy Award nominations. Just as important, it would be a smash at the box office— the kind of success that could help even one of the supporting players begin his ascent back to the top of the Hollywood heap.

The Reeves returned home at the end of October 1992, in time to see Bill Clinton and Al Gore capture the White House. For Chris, who had campaigned hard for the ticket, the victory meant easy access to the powers that be in Washington. On environmental issues in particular, Chris would make use of this newfound access, phoning the White House directly and getting answers to his questions from deputy cabinet members.

Dana was, by all accounts, every bit as passionate about the issues as her husband was. "Whenever I'm a little reluctant to pick up the phone and call," he said, "Dana is right there urging me to do it." Mrs. Reeve made no apologies for giving Superman a nudge now and then. "Chris is a very polite guy, and sometimes he doesn't want to appear pushy. That's where I come in. What's the point of having influence," she asked, "if you don't *use* it?"

In the wake of *The Remains of the Day,* Chris also had a little more clout in Hollywood. After attending the inaugural festivities in Washington, he packed up the family and headed for New Mexico to begin filming the comedy *Speechless* with Michael Keaton and Geena Davis. In the film, based loosely on the romance of flamboyant Clinton spin doctor James Carville and his equally outspoken Republican counterpart Mary Matalin, Chris played an outlandishly narcissistic TV news correspondent.

As they did every year, Chris and Dana launched the *Sea Angel* the first weekend in April, and headed up the coast to Martha's Vineyard with Will in tow. That summer, the Reeves were on the road again—this time to Calgary, Alberta, where Chris played the part of a former plantation owner turned Indian-fighting Texas pioneer in the three-part CBS western miniseries *Black Fox*. This time, thirteen-year-old Matthew and Alexandra, nine, were cast in nonspeaking parts—he as a sheriff's deputy and she as a farmer's daughter.

The movie, not surprisingly, called for Chris to do a lot of riding—not to mention all of his own stuntwork. "Chris is such a total pro," said *Black Fox* producer Les Kimber. "When he says he can do something, no matter how impossible it seems, he always delivers. Chris puts his heart and soul into everything he does."

This summer spent in the Canadian Rockies would hold cherished memories for Chris and Dana. As they swam, rode, played tennis, and hiked (with one-year-old Will strapped on Dad's back) along steep mountain trails together, the Reeves behaved like any other American family on vacation. Matthew and Al were, in Chris's words, "completely smitten" with their little brother—and vice versa.

When Will began taking his first tentative steps, his brother and sister were on hand to cheer him on. Like any doting siblings, they even competed for their little brother's attention. It never mattered that they spent most of the year separated by an ocean, Chris said. "They picked up right where they left off. They never took each other for granted the way other brothers and sisters might," he observed. "Their time together was that much more precious."

Dana, Chris allowed, was "the heart and soul" of their blended family. "She is such a naturally positive person," he said, "that kids are just drawn to her. I know I'm prejudiced, but it's impossible not to like her. And, from a kid's perspective especially, she's *fun*. Dana's a joy to be around."

Still, their Canadian idyll was not without its moments. Chris, who was thrilled to do all his own riding and stunts in *Black Fox,* also insisted on competing in equestrian events in and around Calgary. By this time, having worked with such top teachers as Mike Huber, Yves Sauvignon, Brian Sabo, and Mark Weiss-becker, Chris felt confident enough to compete in combined training events—three-phase competitions that included dressage, stadium jumping, and cross-country jumping. It helped that his allergy to horses—which had required Chris to take frequent stiff doses of the decongestant Dimetapp—seemed to have vanished.

Kristen Hyduchak, who had tried to teach him the basics years before, still worried about the way Chris carried himself on horseback. "I saw him in photos and videos," she said, and was surprised to see that he was still shifting his weight too far for-ward. "That's a recipe for disaster."

Why, then, was Chris competing at such a high level? "When someone comes into your barn with a lot of money," Hyduchak explained, "you tell him, 'What would you like to do?'—whether or not he's well suited for it. You let him do it anyway, because you don't want to lose the prestige and the money." In Chris's case, she told herself at the time, "This is an accident waiting to happen."

Hyduchack was proved right during one of the competitions Chris entered in Calgary that summer of 1993. Chris was about to jump his horse over a ditch when it stopped abruptly, sending Chris hurtling straight ahead—"like a field goal through the horse's ears," he laughingly recalled. Toppling forward, Chris ac-tually did a somersault over the horse's head, landing on his knees. A gasp of horror went up from the crowd. "People watching went

'Ooh!,'" he remembered, but Chris quickly scrambled to his feet, "none the worse for wear."

Not all the dangers Chris confronted involved riding. That same year, Chris did not take Dana and the kids along when he journeyed to Kenya to scout locations for a film he was interested in making, *The Hunt*. In the process, he contracted a serious case of malaria. Once Chris managed to reassure a concerned Dana that he would make a complete recovery, she briefly adopted a new nickname for her husband. Dana began calling him "Indiana Jones."

A few months later, Chris was taking his small plane for a spin above the English countryside when a sudden storm forced him to crash-land in a clearing not far from the Gloucestershire village of Watlington. Amazingly, Chris walked away without a scratch. Dusting himself off, he made his way to the nearest house and knocked on the door. When Chris asked the woman who answered if he could use her phone to call for help, she let him inside.

"Pardon me," she said, studying his face carefully, "but you seem so familiar . . . Have we met?"

"Oh," Chris answered as he dialed the phone. "I'm Superman."

News of yet another brush with death was something Dana had learned to take in stride. She was married to a man who enjoyed living on the edge, and she wasn't about to ask him to stop now. "Chris isn't reckless, but he loves life, and danger is a part of life," she once explained, adding that Chris's exploits were "part of what makes him who he is, and part of the reason I love him. He's an exciting guy."

No less important to Dana was Chris's commitment to the

causes they both believed in. Coming on the heels of sweeping Republican victories in the 1994 congressional elections, the National Endowment for the Arts was more vulnerable than ever. As the newly elected co-president (with Blair Brown) of the Creative Coalition, Chris spearheaded the group's efforts to oppose cuts in NEA funding. According to those who knew them, Dana never complained that Chris's various causes were taking him away from the family. On the contrary, said one longtime family friend, "Dana knew Chris loved what he was doing. She wasn't going to get in the way of that. She believed in him totally, totally."

Reeve family fun resumed in the summer of 1994 when everyone joined Dad in Point Reyes, a seaside village just north of San Francisco, for the filming of *Village of the Damned*. In this remake of the 1960 horror classic starring George Sanders, Chris played a doctor who discovers he is the only person who can destroy the cute-but-murderous alien children who have invaded his small town.

While his own brood played with some of the child actors on the set, Chris found it difficult to see them as evil once the cameras started rolling. "They were so sweet and adorable," he sighed. "They wanted to play Frisbee and sing songs, and I had to look upon them as an alien force."

For the past fifteen years that was precisely the way Hollywood had viewed Reeve. Now, in the wake of those character parts in films like *The Remains of the Day* and *Speechless,* Superman had begun to loosen his grip on Chris's career. Gary Arnold of the *Washington Times* compared Chris to another forty-something whose career had recently taken off after sputtering for years. "It's only a matter of time before Reeve is 'officially' rediscovered and cel-ebrated," Arnold wrote, "like John Travolta in *Pulp Fiction*."

There was still the occasional career disappointment—in 1994 Chris auditioned for the lead in *Jefferson in Paris* but lost it to Nick Nolte. But he could always count on Dana, who balanced her own auditions with raising their two-year-old son, to keep everything in perspective. "It's been tough on her," he acknowledged to one of their closest friends. "She is so talented, but she's hasn't had that big break yet. Mine came so early for me, I think maybe it's a bless-ing when it comes a little later. When Dana gets that breakthrough part, she'll be huge."

In the meantime, she did not underestimate how important it was to spend quality time with Will. The Reeves did employ a full-time nanny and occasionally relied on relatives to look after Will when they both had appointments in New York. But for the most part, it was Dana who drove the ten miles to watch him frolic with the other toddlers enrolled in his Gymboree play group, or to don a swimsuit with the other mothers who brought their kids to Wa-ter Babies in the nearby town of Mt. Kisco.

Chris also took Will to Water Babies whenever he could. Dur-ing those classes and whenever they happened to be staying at a hotel with a pool, Dad made a point of standing in the water, arms outstretched, and coaxing his justifiably wary little boy to jump in. "Trust me, Will," he insisted. "I won't let anything happen to you. Come on." Such reassurances aside, after months in the Water Babies program Will was still refusing to make the leap of faith.

For his part, Chris was grateful for the time with his wife and son—each day Dad now plopped Will on his lap at the piano and encouraged him to pound on the keyboard—as well as the acting jobs that were still coming his way. Not long after losing *Jefferson in Paris,* Chris was offered the lead in the Hallmark Entertainment production *Kidnapped,* Robert Louis Stevenson's classic story of a young man's adventures with a band of eighteenth-century renegade Scots. The four-hour television movie, which was being produced by Francis Ford Coppola for the Family Channel, was set to start shooting in Ireland the following June. Chris relished the idea that, once again, he would be called upon to do some serious riding in the film.

Not long after, Chris was approached by his old friends Ismail Merchant and James Ivory with another screen project. At most, he was hoping they would hand him another juicy supporting role in a sprawling period piece similar to *The Remains of the Day.* They did offer him a role in their next feature, *The Proprietor,* but this time it was the male lead opposite French screen idol Jeanne Moreau.

Chris made use of the time between shoots perfecting his riding skills. While he was filming *Village of the Damned* back in Northern California, Chris had spent $20,000 on a new jumper—a twelve-year-old chestnut gelding named Eastern Express. Buck, as everyone called the horse, combined years of experience in all phases of competition riding with a docile nature.

Buck was certainly not the only horse that Chris had forged an intense bond with. Another favorite was his Irish Thoroughbred, Denver. At the Area 1 Championships in Vermont that September, Chris had actually ridden Denver to an impressive third-place finish. Still, a couple of months later Chris withdrew in the middle of a competition when, after a few successful jumps, he sensed that something was wrong with Denver. "Sorry," Chris told officials as he bowed out, "but he's keeping his head down for some reason, and I'm not going to take any chances." In matters of this nature, Chris like to quote a piece of advice he received from his first flying instructor: "The outcome of any maneuver must never be seriously in doubt."

For all his talents, Denver did have the unfortunate habit of periodically knocking down rails as he jumped—the kind of mistake Chris could not afford if he was going to move up in the sport. Buck, in contrast, was more consistent—a dauntless competitor, particularly when it came to jumping. Once he completed *Village of the Damned,* Chris returned to Bedford with Buck in tow. Dana took an instant liking to the horse, and Chris would hold Will up so he could feed Buck carrots or the occasional sugar cube. "This horse is a winner, right, boy?" Chris said as he stroked Buck's neck. "You and me—we're going places."

Chris spent the late fall and winter months of 1994 for the most part away from Dana and Will, filming his next project, *Above Suspicion,* on location in Los Angeles. In the HBO thriller, he was cast as a police officer who is shot in the line of duty and paralyzed from the waist down. Confined to a wheelchair, the cop, who also happens to have a young son, first entertains thoughts of suicide. Later, he becomes a murder suspect when his wife (played by a pre–*Sex and the City* Kim Cattrall) and his brother, who have been carrying on a clandestine affair, turn up dead.

Years earlier, before playing the part of a double amputee on Broadway in *Fifth of July,* Chris had researched his role by visit-

ing VA hospitals. For *Above Suspicion,* he spent time at a rehabilitation facility in the L.A. suburb of Van Nuys. There he learned
how to use a "sliding board" to make the switch from hospital
bed to wheelchair and then, using only his arms, to maneuver
himself from his wheelchair into a car and back out again.

Much of his time at the rehab hospital in Van Nuys was spent
with victims of the recent Northridge earthquake, many of
whom had been crushed by falling debris. He was particularly
touched by a twenty-five-year-old woman who had suffered severe spinal injuries after being struck on the head by a falling
bookcase. A steel halo held her skull in place, and she had yet to
regain any feeling or movement in her legs. She was, understandably, emotionally as well as physically devastated, and not yet
able—or willing—to accept her condition.

On the phone to Dana from the rehab center, Chris choked
back tears as he told her how the young woman and several other
patients at the rehab center were struggling against the odds to
take even a few halting steps. "Jesus, Dana," Chris said, "it's so
hard to even watch these poor people. Some of them are just
kids—you know, one day they're riding their bikes or shooting
hoops and the next . . . You just think that this can happen to
anybody at any time, you know?"

Dana sympathized. But as the self-confessed "grounded one"
in the relationship, it often fell to her to keep Chris in a positive frame of mind. "Remember that you're there for a reason,"
she told him. "Millions of people are going to learn about what
paralyzed people go through because of your character in the
movie."

Chris took solace in Dana's words, and kept his focus on doing the job he was there to do. But each day when he left the rehab facility, Chris got into his rented car, turned on the ignition, and muttered the same words to himself before heading for the Sunset Marquis Hotel. "Boy," he sighed, shaking his head, "thank *God* that's not me."

"It was as if I'd been hanged,
cut down, and sent to a hospital."
—*Chris*

"You're still *you,* and I will
love you."
—*Dana*

"Without Dana, I doubt if Chris
would have lasted more than a
few days."
—*Dr. John Jane,*
Chris's surgeon

"It saddens me sometimes that
just when everything had come together,
I went out and ruined it."

—*Chris*

"When there's very little to hold on to,
you need an absolute and complete
faith in something. For us, it was love."

—*Dana*

4

March 17, 1995
Bedford, New York

An unseasonably late snowstorm had swept through the Northeast the week before, leaving behind a glistening blanket of white around the Reeves' contemporary Westchester County farmhouse. While outside all was pristine tranquility, inside Chris and Will were cheering Dana on as she blew out the thirty-four candles on her birthday cake and then began tearing through a mountain of presents.

When she got to Chris's gift, Dana paused a moment. "What's this?" she asked, looking at the illustration on the box. "A birdhouse?"

Chris acted just a little wounded at the suggestion that he would ever give her anything so mundane. "No, it's a *butterfly* house," he answered in a mock-scolding tone. Then he pointed to the packet of wildflower seeds that was also in the box. "You see, you plant these seeds around the butterfly house, and when they bloom, they'll attract all the butterflies."

The butterfly house was fairly typical of the kinds of gifts Chris and Dana exchanged—modest but ingenious items that were often a reflection of their abiding love of nature and the environment. Dana was delighted. Chris installed the butterfly house on a post in the yard, and a few weeks later, Dana planted the wildflower seeds in the hard, acidic soil at its base. She didn't have the heart to tell her husband what she really thought—that the seeds "didn't have a chance in hell" of ever sprouting.

Still, each day when she returned from auditions in New York, Dana knelt down to check how the garden was doing. And each day, she saw not even the slightest hint of life.

That first week in April, the Reeves set sail on their annual shakedown cruise aboard the *Sea Angel.* As they edged up the coast toward Cape Cod, a blizzard caught them by surprise. "Chris was in heaven," Dana later recalled, although the increasingly choppy seas were having their usual effect on her. Their visibility reduced to zero by the blinding white storm, Chris steered the *Sea Angel* while Dana kept frantically brushing the snow off the instruments so he could read them. As it happened, her sense of direction was as bad as his was acute. Eventually, Chris and Dana agreed on what they called "The Dana Rule": Whichever way instinctively seemed right to her, Dana conceded, "just go in the opposite direction."

Since they still regarded June 30—the day they met—as the most important date in their relationship, Dana and Chris really hadn't done much to mark their first two wedding anniversaries. For their third, on April 11, they both agreed it was time to pull out the stops. Leaving Will at home in Bedford with the nanny, Mr. and Mrs. Reeve checked into a $1,200-a-night suite at one of their favorite hotels—The Mark on East 77th Street—and then went out to dinner followed by a Broadway show.

Over dinner that night, they agreed the time was right to have a second child. They planned to conceive a little sibling for Will that June in Ireland, when Chris would be on location filming *Kidnapped*. "Just talking about it," Chris later said, "got us, well, worked up."

Their third anniversary would, in fact, turn out to be a passionate replay of the night Chris and Dana decided to get married and celebrated by heading for bed. This time, they returned to their suite at The Mark and made love until dawn. Dana would later use the same word to describe this night that she'd used to describe that other passionate all-night affair: "Magical."

In early May, Chris flew to Ireland and picked out a cottage on the outskirts of Dublin where the Reeves would live—and, if all went according to plan, add to the family—while he made *Kidnapped*. More obsessed than ever with riding, Chris also hired one of Ireland's most respected trainers to work with him.

That spring as he and Dana juggled several responsibilities, Chris somehow found time to lobby for the NEA in Washington and to pose for a safety poster. The poster, intended for distribution by the United States Combined Training Association, showed Chris jumping Denver over a fence. The caption: "In films I've played an invincible hero. But in real life, I wouldn't think of riding without a helmet."

Chris now pinned all his hopes as a competitive rider on Buck. Six days a week he got up before dawn and drove to the nearby stables where Buck was boarded. The hours of training and practice paid off. On May 14, 1995, Dana and Will were among the spectators as Dad and Buck turned in a thrilling performance at the spring horse trials in Southampton, Massachusetts. Feeling more secure on Buck than he had on any other horse ("It's the perfect partnership," he told his longtime coach), Chris signed up for a Memorial Day weekend competition in Vermont.

But then another offer came along. Several other riders who trained with Chris's first coach, Bill McGuinness, were going to Culpeper, Virginia, instead that holiday weekend. They were competing as a group—something that always appealed to the gregarious Chris—and Reeve was asked if he'd like to tag along. Happy to have the company, Chris pulled out of the Vermont competition and managed to sign up for Culpeper with only minutes to spare before the deadline.

Dana was not amused. She and Chris had been apart the last few Memorial Day weekends, and what she wanted was time alone with her husband. Now Chris would drive down with the others on Friday and check into the local Holiday Inn. Dana and Will would join him at the hotel later in the day. "Next Memorial Day," she said, "*I* get to choose what we do."

Chris knew Culpeper well. He had been there before—not to compete, but to scout for Thoroughbreds he might add to his stable. Nestled at the base of the Blue Ridge Mountains, between the Rappahannock and Rapidan rivers, Culpeper was at the epicenter of Virginia horse country. This time, Chris was scheduled to compete at the spring horse trials of the Commonwealth

Dressage and Combined Training Association, held at the two-hundred-acre Commonwealth Park equestrian facility.

At six-foot-four and 215 pounds, Chris was by all accounts simply too big to make it to the front ranks of U.S. equestrians. Yet, ever the competitor, he was hell-bent on going as far as he could in the sport. Arriving in the early afternoon of Friday, May 26, Chris headed straight for Commonwealth Park to rehearse the dressage course with Buck. When he was finished, Chris walked the cross-country course on which he and Buck would also be competing—twice—before settling in with Will and Dana back at the Holiday Inn.

Whenever they were on the road as a family, Mom and Dad always made sure that Will slept in his own room. After an early room service dinner, they turned in for the night, but there would be no opportunity for intimacy, since the door to Will's adjacent room was propped open so they could hear him if he woke up in the middle of the night.

Chris and Buck showed up on time the next morning to compete in the dressage phase of the competition. Proudly showing his own colors—the silver and blue of his prep school alma mater, Princeton Day—Chris donned helmet and padded safety vest, then put Buck through his paces.

Dressage was not Buck's best event—he excelled at cross-country—but he did well nonetheless. When it was over, Chris had placed fourth out of twenty-seven. He returned to the Holiday Inn, where Dana had decided to spend the day with Will; she planned to be among the spectators when he competed in the final event—show jumping—on Sunday. "You know, I think I might actually win this thing," Chris told his wife. "All it takes is for somebody else to make a few mistakes. And the way Buck's been riding, I think we really have a shot."

Dana, no stranger to the equestrian world, was proud that her husband, who had taken up the sport seriously just a decade earlier, had come so far in a relatively short period of time. "Most people start out riding as kids and never get to the point where Chris is," she said. "He is the most focused person I've ever known. When Chris feels passionately about something, he makes anything seem possible."

Chris roughhoused with Will for a while, and then drove back to the equestrian grounds at one-thirty. For the next hour, he carefully studied the cross-country course a third time. Chris was concerned about a couple of jumps—one into and out of water, the other over a bench—but they were toward the end of the course. At least he and Buck would be able to build up a rhythm during the first half dozen jumps, none of which seemed the slightest bit difficult.

A fellow rider and friend of Chris's, John Williams, dropped by to wish him luck before he headed for the warm-up area. It was the last thing Chris would remember for the next four days.

At their precisely scheduled start time of 3:01 P.M., Chris and Buck—Entry No. 103—were off. The first two jumps went smoothly. "The rhythm was fine and Chris was fine, and they were going at a good pace," observed Lisa Reid, a veteran trainer who was among the spectators that day. As they approached the third fence, a three-foot-two-inch-high split rail set in a zigzag pattern—in terms of difficulty, merely a three on a scale of one to ten—Reid was impressed with how seamlessly horse and rider meshed. They were, she said, "coming into the fence beautifully."

Buck started to jump, but then, without warning, abruptly—and disastrously—changed his mind. "The horse put his front feet over the fence, but his hind feet never left the ground," Reid said. "Chris is such a big man. He was going forward, his head over the top of the horse's head. He had committed his upper body to the jump. But the horse—whether it chickened out or felt Chris's weight over its head, I don't know. But the horse decided, 'I can't do this.' And it backed off the jump."

As he had done two years earlier in Calgary, Chris pitched forward and started to slide down the horse's neck. Only this time, Chris's hands were tangled in the reins, and as he soared forward—Buck was putting his head down to avoid Chris's weight—he pulled the bridle, bit and all, off Buck's head.

Unable to break his fall with hands that were tangled up in the horse's tack, Chris hurtled straight ahead, striking his head on the top rail, just under the rim of his helmet. Then he plowed forehead-first into the ground on the other side of the fence, flipping over and snapping his neck in the process. As Chris lay there, motionless, the judge announced over the loudspeaker, "Superman is down!"

Buck backed away, then bolted for the stables. Chris, meanwhile, turned ashen. Although there was no way of assessing the damage at the time, Chris's first and second vertebrae were shattered. It was roughly equivalent to the spinal injury suffered when someone is hanged.

Seconds after Chris hit the ground, one of the spectators heard him say, "I can't breathe." But by the time Helmut Boehme, one of the organizers of the event, arrived one minute later, Chris was unconscious and his lips were turning blue. "He was not moving, he was not breathing," Boehme said. It seemed, he added, as if "the life had gone out of him."

It was three minutes before paramedics arrived on the scene. One dropped to his knees immediately and began giving Chris mouth-to-mouth resuscitation. Within a minute, he was breathing—though barely. Regaining consciousness, he was soon in an agitated state. Turning his head back and forth, Chris demanded to be let alone as emergency medical workers—aided by a woman anesthesiologist who happened to be among the spectators that day—squeezed air into him using a handheld device called an ambu bag.

Stabilizing his neck with a collar, the paramedics carefully lifted Chris onto a stretcher and carried him to a waiting ambulance. Then, rather than cause further damage by jostling the patient, the ambulance drove off the field at a snail's pace.

Dana was still waiting for Will to stir from his afternoon nap when the phone rang in her room at the Holiday Inn. It was 3:20, and she thought for a moment that Chris might have finished early and was calling with good news about his performance. She realized she was wrong the instant she heard the strange voice at the other end of the line. It was Peter Lazar, one of the riders who had driven down from New York with Chris to compete.

"Now, don't panic," Lazar told Dana.

Her heart sank. Before Dana could say anything, Lazar continued, "Chris had a spill." She could already tell by his measured tone and the careful parsing of words that this was more than a sprained wrist. "I don't know why," Lazar said mysteriously, "but they had to take him off in a stretcher."

Dana was not prone to panic, although she knew she had to be at her husband's side. She approached the situation the way she approached everything in life: methodically, and with confidence. She scooped Will out of bed, asked for directions to the hospital, and drove herself there.

Carrying Will into the emergency room, Dana was surprised at how quiet everything seemed; she was, with the exception of one woman whose adolescent son was having a relatively minor cut stitched up, the only person in the waiting room.

"Hi, I'm Dana Reeve," she said to one nurse who passed by. "My husband is here."

"Oh, OK," the nurse answered matter-of-factly.

"Is my husband all right? Is he OK?"

The nurse looked at her blankly. "The doctor," she said calmly, "will be out in a minute."

She would not have to hear from the doctor to realize that something was terribly wrong. Outside the waiting room, Dana had a clear view of a white-and-red medical helicopter with the name "Pegasus" emblazoned on the side landing in the parking lot. "Look, Mommy," Will said, pointing to the helicopter. "A horsy with *wings!*"

The young emergency room doctor on duty, William Maloney, had already ordered that Chris be airlifted the forty-five miles to the University of Virginia Medical Center in Charlottesville. As the chopper waited, Dana, still holding on tight to Will, was escorted to Dr. Maloney's office. With Will sitting in her lap and playfully "honking" Mommy's nose, Dana was told the grim news: Chris had broken his neck, and only a respirator was keeping him alive. If he had any chance for survival, he would require the kind of cutting-edge care that only a major medical facility like UVA Medical Center could provide. With each new, devastating statement about Chris's condition, Dana merely nodded. By the time the doctor was finally finished running down the list of injuries and what they meant, Dana felt as if she had just been worked over in a boxing ring. All the while Will, oblivious to what was going on, kept honking Mommy's nose.

There was no guarantee that Chris would even survive the helicopter trip. "Perhaps you should see your husband now," Dr. Maloney told Dana. She knew what they were saying, but she had Will with her and did not want to upset the little boy. She handed Will to a nurse, and was taken to the room in intensive care where Chris was hooked up to a ventilator. According to a member of the hospital staff, Dana was "wide-eyed, obviously in shock, and it looked like she might just keel over. But then she put her hand on his shoulder, whispered 'I love you,' took a deep breath, and walked away."

Dana called the one man she always relied on for sound medical advice: her dad. When she told him that Chris had broken his neck, Chuck Morosini did not even try to conceal his anxiety. "Oh God," he blurted out. But his concern was also tempered by a belief that, with the best medical care, Chris was young and strong enough to overcome the odds. "Look, honey," he told his daughter, "if anyone can beat this, it's Chris."

Dana certainly believed it. For now, however, she had a job to do. She and Will had to be there when Chris regained consciousness at the UVA Medical Center. Dana had her own coping method for situations like these, although she had to admit to herself that there had never really been a time quite like this. Rather

than crumbling, she merely dealt with the situation head-on—
calmly, efficiently, and without complaint. She carried Will to her
rental car, drove back to the Holiday Inn, then packed up their
things and checked out. She even managed a wan smile for an insistent fan who wanted to have her picture taken with Dana. She
then strapped Will into his car seat and drove the forty-five miles
to UVA.

During the drive, Dana prayed that Chris would survive his
injuries. When she got to the hospital around four-thirty, she was
taken aside by emergency room doctor Mohan Nadkarni.

"I had to break the news of what had happened," Nadkarni
said. "Dana was amazing. She was clearly upset but kept herself
together. She was horrified, but she never broke down."

"Mo," as he insisted on being called, told her that Chris had
been taken to an intensive care unit on the sixth floor in the hospital's west wing. Mo thought Dana needed to know that there
was a chance Chris might never again breathe on his own. For
whatever reason, this was even harder to take than the news that
Chris might die from his injuries. Dana reeled backward, then
steadied herself.

Dana's father was among the first to arrive at the hospital, and,
according to Dr. Nadkarni, the two discussed whether Dana
would give instructions to stop the ventilator. "They decided they
wouldn't do anything," Nadkarni said, "until Matthew and
Alexandra had had a chance to see their father."

At this point, Dr. Nadkarni offered to spend some time with
Will while Dana saw her husband. Mo and Will became fast
friends, and over the next few days the doctor would frequently
help Dana out by babysitting. Dana walked into the ICU, where

Chris lay unconscious. A metal device was attached to his head, holding it in place to prevent further damage to the spine. She sat down next to her husband, and began singing softly to him. Over the next few days, she would sing some of the songs they liked to harmonize on—including "Red River Valley" and "Home on the Range." Another favorite, which they had taught to Will, was Tom Chapin's "This Pretty Planet."

"It was very moving to hear Dana sing that song," said hospital administrator Rebecca Lewis, who became a close friend of the Reeves. "Her voice had this gentle, soothing quality, yet it almost brought you to tears at the same time."

Even as Dana sang to her comatose husband, family and friends began streaming toward the hospital. Matthew, Alexandra, and their mother, Gae Exton, were all struggling to contain their emotions as photographers snapped them at Heathrow waiting to board a flight bound for the United States. Half siblings, stepsiblings, parents, stepparents, and Chris's brother Ben made their way to Charlottesville. They would provide a bulwark of support, but in the end no one came close to bearing the burden that would be carried by Dana from this moment on.

Dana listened patiently as Dr. John Jane, the hospital's cherub-faced chief of neurosurgery, explained her husband's condition. First, he told her Chris was fortunate to be alive at all. There was apparently no brain damage, but Chris was not out of the woods yet. The next step was an operation to reconnect his skull to his spine. It was something that had never been attempted before, and because there was a real possibility he might not survive the surgery, they needed Dana's consent.

Dana, however, was not about to take Chris's control over his own fate away from him. They would have to wait for Chris to regain consciousness and ask him what course *he* wanted to take. For the next five days, Dana sat by the bed and watched as Chris drifted in and out of consciousness. In addition to singing to him, she sometimes swabbed the inside of his mouth with fruit-flavored swabs—he was permitted no liquids or solids leading up to his possible surgery.

The first few times he regained consciousness, Chris launched into wild-eyed rants about the forces of evil who were out to get him—paranoid delusions caused by the drugs he had been given and the disorienting effect of simply being in the ICU. Chris's bizarre behavior "threw me at first," Dana later said. She worried that they were an indication that Chris might have suffered some sort of brain damage—until doctors explained that such hallucinations were common, and temporary in nature.

Ironically, while a delusional Chris kept urging Dana to "get the gun" so they could fight off intruders, she was actually resisting efforts on the part of one family member to end his suffering. Almost from the moment she was told her son would in all likelihood be totally paralyzed from the neck down and not even be able to breathe on his own—if he survived at all—Barbara Johnson lobbied to have doctors remove Chris from life support.

With every passing hour, Barbara became more and more agitated. "You know Chris wouldn't want to live like this," she told everyone but Dana, who kept repeating that all decisions about his future were to be made by him and him alone. "I don't know why," Barbara went on, "we are doing some of these measures . . ."

Observed one hospital staffer, "Chris's mom was very sweet, but, understandably, she was also very emotional. This was her first-born child."

The argument over whether or not to allow Chris's life to end at this juncture raged on out of Dana's earshot, in hospital corridors and waiting rooms, and at the Omni Hotel in Charlottesville, where the family was staying. Barbara kept pushing the issue, talking directly to Dr. Jane and his deputy, Dr. Scott Henson, and at one point consulting the hospital clergy. No man embraced action and excitement more than Chris. To be strapped, motionless, to a wheelchair for the rest of his life, breathing only with the aid of a machine—this would be a living hell for her son, Barbara argued. The humane thing, she said, would be to end his suffering now. It was what Chris would want.

Finally, Barbara reportedly decided to take matters into her own hands. She announced that, the following day, they were going to take Chris off life support. She was told that perhaps she was letting the emotion of the moment get the better of her, and that now was the time for a little patience. Chuck Morosini was more blunt: Nothing was to be done, he said firmly, without the express consent of his daughter.

When Matthew and Alexandra finally did arrive from England with their mother, Exton walked directly up to Dana and handed her a dozen roses. "I want you to know," Exton said, "that I care deeply for you, too." Dana, moved by the gesture, embraced her husband's former lover.

On Friday, June 1—fully five days after his fall—Chris seemed aware enough of his surroundings to give his consent to the surgery. But first he had to decide whether or not it was worth the effort. Chris later confessed that simple embarrassment over his physical state and the burden it caused for others fueled thoughts of suicide. "Oh, I don't want to cause you people trouble," he would say to Dana, or "I don't want to be a burden."

Barbara Johnson, whom Chris later acknowledged was only acting "out of love" when she lobbied to take him off life support, had correctly anticipated her son's wishes. "At first, Chris wanted to die—no question," Dr. Jane recalled. "He was very insistent about that. He was a smart guy. He knew what was going on. Here was a man who got up every morning wondering whether he was going to sail his yacht or fly his plane or play tennis. Suddenly, he can't move, he can't feel. He didn't feel this new life he was faced with was worth living."

Finally, when he and Dana were alone, Chris confronted the issue head-on. "Maybe," he said to her, "we should let me go."

Dana had been holding everything in until now, for Will's sake. But at this moment, she began to weep. After she regained her composure, she looked Chris in the eye and firmly told him where she stood. "Toph, I am only going to say this once," she said. "I will support whatever you want to do, because this is your life, and your decision. But I want you to know that I'll be with you for the long haul, no matter what . . . You're still *you*. And I love you."

It was the moment that saved Chris's life, and the defining moment in their relationship. There was not the slightest hint of pity in what Dana was saying. She was expressing her love and commitment to him, but also her need for him, and Chris felt it.

Dana did not, however, leave the issue there. She pointed out that he had not suffered brain damage, that once he emerged from the fog of medication he would realize that he was as mentally sharp as ever. But if that wasn't enough, then she made him a proposition: "We should wait for at least two years. Then, if you still feel it's not worth it, we'll both figure out a way to let you go." (Later, Dana would confess that this maneuver was "just, you know, a sales technique.")

Chris smiled wanly. "This is way beyond the marriage vows," he half-joked, "in sickness and in health."

"I know," Dana replied.

Almost from the moment paramedics carried Chris off the field in Culpeper, reporters were frustrated by the lack of information being made available to them. The hospital, bowing to the family's wishes, would only say that Reeve was in "serious but stable" condition. Actually Dana, still trying to sort out the facts herself, had decided the best course for the time being was a news blackout. Toward that end, she asked Chris's publicist Lisa Kasteler to stonewall the press. After Kasteler repeatedly claimed not to know anything about Chris's condition, she was asked just whom she was speaking for—Dana or Chris. Kasteler answered simply, "They are one and the same right now."

At first, some news organizations, left to assume that Reeve had not been seriously injured and was on the mend, basically downplayed the story or ignored it altogether. But as the mystery deepened, more than sixty reporters from around the world descended on Charlottesville looking for answers. Tabloid reporters staked out the hospital and worked their phones, offering cash to hospital employees for inside information. TV camera crews gathered in the parking lot, hoping to corner a family member or doctor. Aware that at least one reporter had been found wandering the hospital corridors in search of Chris, extra security guards were posted at the main entrance and just down the hall from his room.

Guarding Dana would also prove to be a challenge. When it soon became evident that moving from one hotel to another to avoid the paparazzi was pointless, Becky Lewis moved out of her own apartment and turned it over to Dana and Will. Lewis also arranged for two different rental cars to be available each day, so that Dana would never arrive and depart the hospital in the same vehicle.

Dana was far too preoccupied to deal with the demands of a ravenous press. Not only had she been trying to absorb the medical details of her husband's condition, but she had been spending hours by his bedside simply holding his motionless, unfeeling hand and singing to him. And whatever strength she had left she devoted to making things as normal as possible for their son.

The effect all this was having on Will was obvious. In the beginning he was terrified of the big machines that Daddy was hooked up to and the whooshing and beeping sounds they made. In the hospital playroom just a few doors down, he kept falling off the toy horse and yelling that he had broken his neck.

"Well, your neck is OK, but Dad's neck is not," Dana told him. She later recalled that Will "had this fear, as small children do, that he would catch his father's illness or that I would get sick."

Over the course of those few days, it fell to Dana to try to allay her son's anxieties, while holding her own in check. "You see," she told Will as she led him into Chris's room, "Daddy is just lying

down, that's all. All these machines are good guys—they're helping Daddy to breathe."

Reassured, Will went back to the Omni Hotel and did something he never dared to do during all those Water Babies classes
back in Mt. Kisco. With Matthew and Alexandra looking proudly
on, he jumped from the side of the hotel pool without having to
be coaxed. "It was amazing," Dana told Chris later. "Once he con-
quered the fear of your being in the ICU, the other stuff must
have seemed small to him. He wasn't afraid of the water anymore.
He was suddenly this brave little guy who couldn't wait to jump
out as far as he could and to duck his head beneath the surface.
He'd come up for air smiling away."

After four days of relative silence, Dana gave the green light
to a press conference. Dr. Jane was no stranger to television; he
was one of the featured surgeons on the Learning Channel series *The Operation*. Stepping before TV cameras on the morning
of Wednesday, May 31, Jane told the world that Chris "currently
has no movement or spontaneous respiration." Although the
spinal cord had not actually been severed, Jane explained, an operation would soon be required to "stabilize the upper spine."
There was an added complication: Chris was now suffering from
pneumonia, and no surgery could be performed until his lungs
cleared up. Beyond that, Jane added, "it is premature to specu-
late about his long-term prognosis."

Representing Chris's extended family, Ben Reeve stepped forward to extend thanks for "expressions of goodwill from so many
people." (In the end, Chris would receive more than 400,000 letters of support from around the globe.) "We do not know what

lies ahead," Ben said. "It means everything to Christopher to have all your thoughts and good wishes."

The grim news spawned headlines that ran the gamut from lurid to merely shocking. While the *Washington Post* announced "RIDING ACCIDENT PARALYZES ACTOR CHRISTO-PHER REEVE," the full-page headlines in the *New York Post* went from "VIGIL FOR SUPERMAN: FAMILY GATHERS AS MYSTERY DEEPENS OVER STRICKEN ACTOR" to "SU-PERMAN PARALYZED: HE MAY NEVER WALK AGAIN." The New York *Daily News* blared "BROKEN DREAMS: OUT-LOOK GRIM FOR SUPERMAN STAR." The title of *People* magazine's cover story waxed more poetic: "FALLEN RIDER—AN ACCIDENT LEAVES CHRISTOPHER REEVE FIGHT-ING FOR HIS LIFE."

The family and hospital staff did what they could to protect Dana from the news accounts, but it quickly became evident that the effort was futile. News reports on Chris's condition flashed on every TV screen in the hospital, not to mention the front-page stories with headlines like "SUPERMAN'S FIGHT FOR LIFE" and "HOPE SLIM FOR SUPERMAN" that were springing up everywhere. "There was no escaping it," Dana said, "but that was OK. It was nice to know people cared, and I was just too busy dealing with more important things to really dissect everything that was being written."

Dana made sure Chris was shielded from all the mayhem that was going on outside his room. It was frightening enough that he now faced an operation for which there was only a 50 per-cent chance of survival. "I'm so worried about his state of mind,"

Dana confided to one of Chris's doctors. "I know he's terrified and depressed—God, he has every right to be—but I don't want that to hurt his chances of pulling through this."

Dana did what she could to lift his spirits, ushering friends and relatives in (the staff was told to weed out imposters by asking visitors if they knew Dana's nickname for Chris—"Toph"), reading from the thousands of letters of support, and of course bringing Will by to tell Daddy about the day's events. But when he woke up alone after midnight, Chris was left to imagine the worst. All Dana could think of to do was to bring in a bed and sleep alongside him in the room—"so that when he wakes up, I'll be right there."

"They were very clearly a *team*," Dr. Nadkarni said, adding that neither displayed "the sense of entitlement" common to many celebrity patients. "The way she would clap her hand on his shoulder, the way he was always looking at her whenever she was in the room—it was really something."

One morning Dana had stepped away for a few minutes, when, without warning, a doctor wearing a yellow surgical gown, glasses, and a blue scrub hat burst into the room and announced in a thick Russian accent that he was the hospital's chief proctologist. Then, snapping a surgical glove on his hand with a theatrical flourish, he announced that he was there to give Chris an immediate rectal exam.

"I'm just goink to haff to, just go down, hold on . . ."

It was only then that, catching a closer look at the face beneath the glasses, Chris realized that the "chief proctologist" was his old buddy Robin Williams. As Chris wept with laughter—it was the first time he had laughed since winding up in the hospital—Dana and Robin's wife, Marsha, poked their heads into the room. No one knew better than Dana the powerful effect Robin's special brand of manic humor had on Chris. It was her idea for Williams to visit in the days before the operation, and that the visit be a complete surprise.

After Chris had stopped laughing, the two friends talked. "So," Williams asked, half in jest, "what's going on?"

"Well, there's a big debate going on," Chris mouthed, "about whether or not to pull the plug."

"Yeah?" Williams said.

"But then I saw Dana and Will," Chris struggled to explain, "so I decided to stick around."

Williams tried to remain upbeat, but he also wanted his pal from the days at Juilliard to know that he was there for him. "Chris," he said, "you know I'll do anything for you, man. Anything." On one other occasion, recalled hospital administrator Becky Lewis, Robin's mood turned serious. "Is my friend," Williams asked John Jane, "going to be OK, Doctor?" Otherwise, Williams devoted himself to keeping up his friend's spirits. When basketball legend Shaquille O'Neal sent Chris a pair of his size twenty-two sneakers, Robin hung them up on Chris's IV stand and began praying "to the god of Shaq's shoes."

Dana's strategy worked. Robin Williams's visit gave Chris renewed confidence that he could not only survive but, as Chris later said, "live a life that was worth living."

The kids were a big part of that realization, as well. Whatever thoughts of suicide lingered, they were finally dispelled when Dana sent all three of Chris's children in to see him. "The minute they all came in," Chris remembered, "and I could see the love and feel the love and know that we were still a family and that we're great, and how lucky we all are that my brain is on straight, that thought vanished—and it has never come back."

While Chris lay facedown on the operating table for more than eight hours, Dana kept herself busy with Will in a hospital playroom. When Chris finally emerged from surgery, Dana was shocked at what she saw. His face was bruised and swollen, his eyes reddened slits. The doctors explained that this was the natural result of trauma resulting from the surgery, and that in less than a day his face would return to normal. This time Dana, who had somehow managed to remain stoic even while everyone around her dissolved in tears, was visibly shaken.

She was not the only one. As soon as he could mouth the words, Chris said to Dr. Jane, "I want to thank you for giving me life." Tears were streaming down the surgeon's face when he left the room.

Her husband's battered appearance was not the only thing that pushed Dana over the edge. Will was to turn three the day after his father's surgery, and Dana busied herself ordering the cake, hiring the clown, wrapping presents, and blowing up balloons for the little boy's birthday party at the nearby Boar's Head Inn. By this time, the UVA staff—Becky Lewis, Drs. Jane, Henson, and Nadkarni as well as the nurses and orderlies—were like family to Will, and they brought along other children Will's age to help him celebrate.

"Will had a wonderful time," one of the nurses said. "It was great to see his little face light up when he opened his gifts. But when he opened the ones Dana said were from Daddy, you know, everyone's heart just sort of sank. He'd just come out of surgery and it was still touch and go." Dana "must have been worried out of her mind, but she never let on for one second. You couldn't help but have enormous respect for her."

Dana videotaped the party for Chris, and when he had recovered sufficiently from the operation, she thought she'd surprise him with it. But when he saw strangers singing "Happy Birthday" to his son, Chris began weeping. "It's hard to watch," he mouthed to Dana. "Very hard . . ."

"She was absolutely remarkable from Day One," recalled Dr. Jane. "Dana was *constant*. She played an optimistic, supportive role and was absolutely loving towards him one hundred percent of the time."

Yet over the next few weeks, Chris would endure many dark nights of the soul. He would awake around 2 A.M. when his sedative wore off, and remain alert for the next five hours—time to dwell on the horror of being trapped inside his body, and of the magnitude of the "colossally stupid" mistake he felt he had made. "I'm an idiot, a fool," he thought to himself. "Look what I've done to myself, to Dana, to my whole family." This was, Chris later admitted, the realization of a fear he had harbored for years—that someday the headlines would read "SUPERMAN HIT BY BUS." Now it was really happening, only the headlines were "SUPERMAN IS PARALYZED."

Dana tried her best to help Chris cope with the "demon hours," as he called them. But there was no way she could be with Chris twenty-four hours a day and at the same time care for Will. Nor could she always be on hand to assist her husband when he was faced with a real medical emergency.

One of the things Chris came to fear most was the "pop-off"—when the hose providing him with life-sustaining oxygen simply popped off the ventilator. Once that happens, the patient can survive on his own for no more than three or four minutes. Not able to move or cry out, Chris prayed that the nurses on duty were paying attention to the alarm that sounded and would rush in to reconnect him. Later, while undergoing rehabilitation at another facility, Chris would have his worst experience with a pop-off when a security guard heard the alarm, came in, and then left to get a nurse—wasting precious moments when he could simply have switched on the light and reconnected the hose to the machine.

"The alarm is sounding on my vent," Chris remembered, "and I'm making this clicking noise with my throat—clk, clk, clk—and the security guy comes in and asks, 'Are you all right, Mr. Reeve?' The vent is screaming, and I'm clicking. All he needed to do was put the hose back in place, but I guess his instructions were that his job was security, so he goes off to get a nurse."

That time Chris was gripped by panic as he began to lose consciousness—"I thrashed around . . . I was like a tuna fish landed in a boat, rolling around with the hook still in my mouth"—all before a nurse sprinted to his rescue.

Dana took it upon herself to check on the connections personally—to make sure the nurses had taped the hose securely to the ventilator, and that they were able to respond quickly if an alarm went off. "She was his guardian and protector from the very start," said one staff member. "Dana was never rude or overbearing, but she was on top of every detail when it came to

Christopher's care. She asked lots of questions, and didn't stop until she was satisfied with answers."

Nor was anyone more perturbed than Dana when one newspaper suggested that a suicidal Chris had somehow been responsible for disconnecting the ventilator hose himself. "God," she said when she was shown the story. "Just what is it about the word 'paralyzed' that these people don't understand?"

Once he was out of bed and in a wheelchair, Dana could wheel Chris down the corridor to what she called the "mailroom," the little office the hospital had set up just for her. There, family members sorted through thousands of cards and letters, picking out the ones to read to Chris as he lay in bed. One of those that meant the most to Chris was from his old friend Kate Hepburn. In her typically cryptic fashion, Hepburn had simply written, "Let me know if I can do anything—My golly what a mess." It was enough for Chris. "I know how much she cares," he said. "It's probably overwhelming for her."

Although Dana had every right to be overwhelmed, she refused to allow that to happen. When hospital officials offered the services of a massage therapist on the staff, Dana declined. "I'm afraid if I let go," she told Becky Lewis, "I'll just cry and cry and never stop." Dana "knew she was in a perfect storm," Lewis said, "and she was determined to keep sailing forward."

It was just after five one morning, and as three physical therapists slowly maneuvered Chris into his wheelchair, he was once again turning those agonizing "what if?" thoughts over and over in his mind—"What if I had gone sailing instead? What if I'd kept my hands free and not let them get tangled up in the reins? What if I hadn't leaned so far forward in the saddle?"

Before he could ask where he was going, Chris was being pushed down the hall and into an elevator. Moments later the elevator doors opened, and there was Dana, standing by the window. "Hi, babe," she said, pointing to the view. "Pretty, don't you think?" Suddenly, they were alone—not a nurse or aide in sight. Dana took her husband's unfeeling hand in hers, and together they stared, silently, as the sun rose over the Virginia countryside.

These precious moments would help Chris as he came to the realization that, after the operation, he could still feel nothing below his shoulders. In addition to not being able to move his legs, arms, or hands, Chris could not breathe on his own, or control bladder and bowel movements.

So for the next five weeks, Chris would begin to learn what it was like to have to rely on others for virtually everything. Someone would have to feed him, bathe him, shave him, comb his hair, brush his teeth, and dress him. He would need people to help him urinate and defecate, and then to dispose of his waste. These were painful, often humiliating and even degrading aspects of his new life, but Chris realized he had no choice but to face them and move on.

In the meantime, only those few hours each night when he could manage some sleep provided him with some form of escape. It was then that he dreamt he was sailing to Nantucket, or flying solo across the Atlantic, or skiing down a mountainside— or gliding over a fence astride Buck. Or making love to Dana.

The last Wednesday in June, Chris had come far enough to leave the hospital for the Kessler Institute for Rehabilitation in West Orange, New Jersey. Just forty minutes west of Manhattan,

Kessler was one of the country's premier rehabilitation centers for those suffering from severe spinal cord injuries.

Dana had gone ahead to prepare the way. She arranged for Chris to have a private room—room 118, one of the largest and nicest the institute had to offer. Security guards in dark suits and sunglasses had also been provided by the institute to protect their star patient. Dana had put up a poster of the space shuttle *Discovery* lifting off the launchpad at Cape Canaveral. "We found nothing is impossible" was scrawled across the top of the poster, along with signatures of each and every NASA astronaut.

Before they left, Dana thanked everyone at the University of Virginia Medical Center for all they had done for Chris. "She was so gracious and grateful and just delightful," Dr. Nadkarni said. "We were all very dazzled by her."

Once Chris was settled in at Kessler, Dana drove herself home to Bedford. She had been gone for six weeks, but it seemed like an eternity. As she got out of the car and walked up the drive toward the front door, Dana choked back the tears. There were the steps that Chris used to take three at a time. There was the lawn where father-and-son games of tag always ended with Daddy tossing Will up in the air and then playfully rolling in the grass.

"It was almost too much to take—just realizing that these things probably weren't ever going to happen again," she later said of that moment. But then, Dana spotted the butterfly house Chris had given her for her birthday. The wildflower seeds that Dana had given up on so long ago had exploded into a riot of purples, pinks, and blues. "Oh, you have got to be kidding!" she said, wiping away a tear. The wildflowers were more than merely beautiful; they had not only survived adversity—they were flourishing.

Dana got on the phone right away and called her husband at Kessler. A nurse put the call on speaker phone. "You remember the butterfly house you bought me for my birthday—and those wildflower seeds?" she asked.

"Sure," Chris replied.

"Well, the wildflowers are out of control! Wildflowers gone wild."

"You're kidding," Chris said. "Gee . . ."

"And there are butterflies *everywhere*." For a moment, there was just silence between them. "We both knew what it meant," Dana later said of the butterfly house and the wildflowers. "It wasn't just about seeds and wildflowers and butterflies. It was a real sign of something we both needed so much at that moment. It was a real sign of hope."

1.

2.

Chris's career took off like, well, a speeding bullet with the release of *Superman* in 1978. In his next film, 1980's *Somewhere in Time*, Reeve traveled back to 1912 to meet the woman of his dreams, played by Jane Seymour. Over the years, *Somewhere in Time* would garner a huge and enthusiastic following not only in the U.S. but throughout the world.

3.

4.

5.

Man of Action: Even before he met Dana, Chris flew his own glider, piloted his own plane solo across the Atlantic, and sailed his own yacht. Also involved in a wide variety of social causes, Chris spoke in 1983 at White House ceremonies marking the fifteenth anniversary of the Special Olympics as Ronald and Nancy Reagan looked on.

6.

7.

Chris and Dana Morosini ham it up during a duet at the Williamstown, Massachusetts Theater Festival Cabaret in July 1987. Only days before, on this same stage, he saw her for the first time— and, Chris recalled, "I went down hook, line, and sinker."

8.

9.

Chris and fellow Juilliard School alumnus Robin Williams—here at a screening in 1987—were, Dana said, "more like brothers than friends." The Reeves were decked out in evening attire for the New York premiere of Robin Williams' film *Awakenings* in 1990.

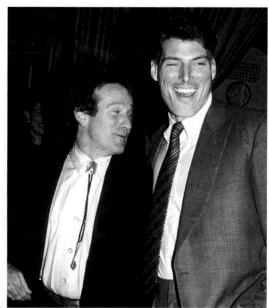

10.

11.

Chris and Dana lace up, then take to the ice in January 1991. He was an expert skater who played varsity hockey at prep school; she was "just holding on to him for dear life."

12.

13.

14.

Chris and Dana headed out for dinner in New York in April 1991, with Matthew, eleven, and seven-year-old Alexandra—Chris's children with British model agent Gae Exton. With her natural, fun-loving manner, Dana instantly won the kids over. After five years together, Dana and marriage-shy Chris finally tied the knot in a small ceremony near Williamstown in April 1992. She gave birth to Will two months later.

15.

16.

Chris and his horse Buck
proved a formidable team
at the King Oak Farm
Horse Trials on May 14,
1995. Less than two weeks
later in Virginia, Buck
would stop short while
making a similar jump—
with tragic consequences
for Chris. Just days after
his accident, Chris was
still clinging to life when
Dana updated the press
on his condition. Later,
at the Kessler Institute
for Rehabilitation, Chris
got his best medicine
from three-year-old Will
—a kiss.

17.

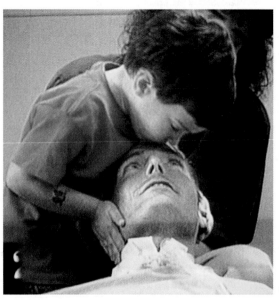

18.

19.

Dana lovingly reassured Chris just minutes before he presented an award to Robin Williams at the annual Creative Coalition dinner on Oct. 17, 1995—his first public appearance after the accident. After his stunning surprise appearance at the 1996 Oscars, Chris and Dana, joined by Robin Williams, congratulated Best Actress winner Susan Sarandon (for *Dead Man Walking*) at the Governor's Ball that followed.

20.

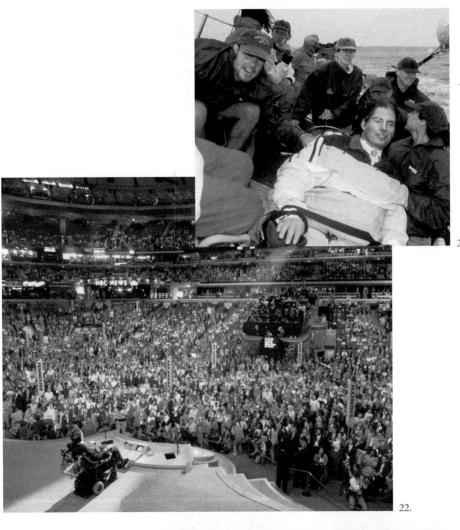

21.

22.

Back in Action: With Dana taking the helm behind him, Chris and his wheelchair had to be literally strapped to the deck when he returned to the sea in the summer of 1996. Not long after, he brought the crowd to its feet when he addressed the Democratic National Convention in Chicago. During this same period, he directed his first film, the critically acclaimed HBO drama *In the Gloaming*, starring Glenn Close.

23.

Paul Newman got the joke when Dana playfully covered Chris's eyes at a party following her October 1998 Broadway debut in *More to Love*. But Will, at Daddy's side, didn't seem too sure. A month later Dana and Chris were all smiles as they joined (from left) Blair Brown, Ted Danson, Ron Silver, Alec Baldwin, Mary Steenburgen, and Billy Baldwin at the Creative Coalition's Spotlight Awards dinner.

24.

25.

26.

27.

28.

In July 2002, ten-year-old Will and his mom watched the action during the Karrie Webb Celebrity Pro-Am Golf Tournament in Purchase, New York. "He has a resiliency," Dana said of Will, "very much like his dad." Will took it in stride when his father, suffering from alopecia and side effects from his medication, decided to go totally bald—a look he sported at the Tonys in June 2003. The following year, Chris and Dana shared the stage as co-commencement speakers at Dana's alma mater, Vermont's Middlebury College.

29.

30.

The program for Chris's memorial service at Juilliard featured a photo of the young Reeve doing one of the things he loved best: sailing. Just eleven days following her husband's death in October 2004, Dana carried on Chris's work, campaigning for stem-cell research supporter John Kerry in Columbus, Ohio. Not long after, she and Will attended the annual Christopher Reeve Foundation "Magical Evening" fundraiser in New York. Over the following year, Dana's mother would die suddenly, Dana would be diagnosed with lung cancer, and her father would suffer a stroke.

31.

No one realized that Dana, still undergoing chemotherapy, was wearing a wig when she playfully posed with Robin Williams at the Reeve Foundation's "Magical Evening" fundraiser in November 2005. On January 12, 2006, New York Ranger and Reeve family friend Mark Messier applauded as a healthy-looking Dana belted out "Now and Forever" at Madison Square Garden ceremonies marking Messier's retirement. Dana died less than eight weeks later. She was forty-four.

32

33

34.

Carrying on: Matthew, twenty-seven, Alexandra, twenty-three, and fifteen-year-old Will—who lost his parents and his beloved grandmother in the span of less than eighteen months—paid tribute to Chris and Dana at the renamed Chris and Dana Reeve Foundation's annual "Magical Evening" in November 2007. His parents, said a close friend, gave Will "the gift of bravery and grace."

35.

"Dana saved my life."

—*Chris*

"Here comes your medication, mon."

—*Jamaican hospital aide*
"Juice" Miller to Chris
whenever Dana walked
into the room

"Without Dana, I couldn't do any of this.
Without the kids, I couldn't do any
of this. They're my reason to push
and keep going."

—*Chris*

"Daddy can't move. But he can
still smile."

—*Will*

5

—————

Dana leaned over to wipe the spaghetti sauce off Will's chin. They had said good night to Chris at six-thirty—his prescribed bedtime during recovery—and now they were sitting at a front window table in West Orange's Eagle Rock Diner. "It was fun seeing Daddy today, wasn't it?" she asked.

"Yes," Will nodded emphatically. "It was."

They had no way of knowing that, back at Kessler, doctors and nurses were scrambling in a frantic effort to save Chris's life. This time, he had suffered a reaction to a new spinal cord regeneration drug and gone into anaphylactic shock. His breathing stopped, and for a few moments Chris was floating above his body, watching as everyone worked over what appeared to be his lifeless form—the classic out-of-body experience.

Then one of the doctors administered epinephrine, and Chris was suddenly jolted back into his body. Gasping for breath, he was lifted onto a stretcher and taken by ambulance to St. Barnabas Hospital in nearby Livingstone.

"Look!" Will yelled to his mother, pointing out the restaurant window. "An ambulance!"

"Yes, that's an ambulance all right," Dana said, wincing as the sound of the siren pierced the night air. "Now finish your dinner." It was only when she returned to Kessler to check up on Chris before going home to Bedford that she learned that the ambulance that had sped by the restaurant was carrying her husband.

Rushing to St. Barnabas, Dana was taken to intensive care. There, she saw Glenn "Juice" Miller, one of Chris's favorite physical therapy aides, sitting at her husband's bedside. Nicknamed Juice by the Kessler staff because of his talent for whipping up phenomenal tropical fruit smoothies in a blender, Miller had been badly shaken by Chris's brush with death. When Dana arrived, they were both overcome with emotion. "It was a close call," he told her in a thick Jamaican accent. "A real close call."

Incredibly, Chris, determined to be able to withstand the drug that might repair damage to his spine, asked to be given a second dose. He promptly began to go into shock again, and was quickly brought back with yet another injection of epinephrine.

Just a few days earlier, Chris and Dana had toasted the eighth anniversary of their first meeting in Williamstown with fruit juice. "We really had no idea," she said, "of what Chris still faced."

There would soon be other medical emergencies, as Chris learned just how all-pervasive a spinal cord injury could be. Bedsores were a constant problem; one eventually grew to the size of a fist and penetrated to the bone. There were times when a kink in his catheter or a bowel obstruction sent his blood pressure soaring, bringing him perilously close to a heart attack or stroke. His sweat glands no longer worked properly, so just a few too many minutes in the sun could result in heatstroke.

Beyond the poking and prodding by doctors, the endless tests, and the hours upon hours of physical therapy, even the most quotidian tasks suddenly seemed daunting. Eating, for example, was something that would be virtually impossible for the next five months. Having developed an overly strong olfactory sense—not unusual in the case of spinal cord injuries—Chris was sickened by the smell of practically all food. When Dana surprised him with Chinese takeout, he was so nauseated by the smell that, Dana later recalled, "I had to eat it in the bathroom." Until his departure later that year, Chris remained on a feeding tube implanted directly into his stomach.

Being moved from the bed to his wheelchair yielded new anxieties for Chris. When Juice and the other aides tried to coax him into his new $40,000 wheelchair for the first time—a maneuver that involved unhooking him from the ventilator on his bed and hooking him up to the one on the chair—he was gripped by fear. He could not shake the idea that somehow the transfer might not work—that he would black out before he could be reattached to the ventilator on the chair.

No matter what Dana said to try to reassure him, Chris was inconsolable. That he should suddenly become so upset about something so innocuous baffled her—until she realized that he was still feeling the effects of having almost died from anaphylactic shock. "That's what this is all about," she told the doctors. "Chris feels even more vulnerable now than he did after the accident."

Eventually, Dana and Juice would coax Chris into the Quickie P300 model wheelchair, which Chris could control by either blowing into or sipping from a plastic straw. Within a few weeks, he would be zooming through the hallways at Kessler, sending orderlies and doctors alike scattering as he learned to maneuver the vehicle with a few puffs of air.

In the meantime, there were other phobias to overcome. The idea of showering—of placing himself in a situation where he might be helpless to avoid drowning—terrified Chris. One night, he finally relented. But he would only shower if Dana was on hand to make sure nothing went wrong.

"So," Dana announced playfully as she entered the room. "Tonight's the big night!" Juice did the heavy lifting, transferring Chris from the wheelchair into a hammocklike net that would suspend his body under the shower.

Seeing that her husband was still terrified, Dana, fully clothed, stepped inside the shower stall with him. "I want us to take a shower together as much as you do," she cracked, standing out of the spray so that only the bottoms of her pant legs would get wet. "But this is ridiculous!"

Chris managed to laugh. With Dana filling him in on Will's latest antics and Juice regaling him with hospital gossip, Chris was able to keep his mind off the fears that threatened to paralyze him emotionally as well as physically.

They had always been a tactile couple, but now it seemed they touched more than ever. Dana was constantly sidling up to Chris, placing her hand on his shoulder, tousling his hair, nuzzling him or casually draping her arm over his chest, playfully throwing one of her legs over his. In his wheelchair, Chris's paralyzed hands always lay splayed on their black leather rests, but Dana touched and held them constantly.

They were more affectionate than ever, in part because Dana was sure the contact had a therapeutic effect not only on Chris but on her. "I needed the reassurance and the warmth as much as he did," she allowed. "Maybe more." Dana's hands-on approach was also due to the simple fact that any contact now had to be initiated by her. "I was used to Chris drawing me into his arms. Now I had to do all the hand-holding and caressing. I was touching for two."

Dana also helped out with therapy when she could. She would hold her hand against one side of Chris's head as he tried to press against it, or gently massage his shoulders, hands, and feet to maintain healthy circulation. She also brought Will along. Soon he was crawling all over his father and, in Chris's words, "using me like a jungle gym."

"We were careful, of course, that Will didn't disconnect any of his dad's trach tubes or anything by accident," said Chris's long-time physical therapist, Erica Druin. "But Chris and Dana both felt it was important for Will to be comfortable climbing all over his dad—that he not be *afraid*." In fact, Will often took an active part in his father's therapy. "I would be stretching Chris's leg up in the air, and Will would be standing on the mat underneath helping me. He wanted to help so much, and he did. It was always a family effort."

Druin remembered that Dana "wanted to keep everything light and fun." There was a stage at one end of the gym at Kessler, and "music was always playing over the intercom. Will and Dana would climb up on the stage and start singing and dancing around—really hamming it up. Chris laughed so hard. He just loved it."

Chris lived for these visits from Dana and Will. "His face just lit up the minute they walked in," Juice Miller said. "You could see that they meant everything to him. They were his world."

Dana knew this better than anyone, and had completely re-arranged her life so that she could be there for Chris as often as humanly possible. Just before dawn each day, she crept into Will's room to give her sleeping son a kiss on the cheek before leaving him with the nanny. Then she climbed into her black Eagle Vision sedan and drove the eighty-five miles from Bedford to Kessler.

Stopping by the admissions desk on the way in, she picked up some of the hundreds of letters and cards that were arriving for Chris each day. Then Dana perused the day's list of scheduled visitors—usually family members like Ben and his mother, although occasionally celebrity pals like Alec Baldwin and Bobby Kennedy, Jr. (A visit from his old colleague Treat Williams was particularly memorable. When Williams dropped by unannounced, he found Chris sitting in the day room. "Don't get up," he joked.) Once she looked the list over, Dana gently reminded the nurse at the desk not to let anyone in who was not on it.

From there, she took the elevator to the second floor and stopped in at the nurses' station to see if Chris had managed to get a decent night's sleep. Then she would head for Chris's room and give him a good morning kiss before feeding him a breakfast of fresh fruit—the only food he could easily tolerate.

Dana would usually accompany Chris to his first physical therapy session, and then slip away around 11 A.M. just long enough to do a multitude of family errands. Back beside Chris by early afternoon, Dana would push his wheelchair around Kessler's seven-acre grounds. It was, Chris later said, "the high point of my day. No matter how terrible things are, Dana has the power to make it all go away. She just kept, well, saving me. Her love is that strong."

This quickly became evident to literary agent Dan Strone, who journeyed to Kessler to discuss the possibility of representing Chris in a book deal. During the meeting, Chris lay in bed, with Dana sitting on a chair to his right. While the adults talked, Will happily crawled all over his unflappable mom.

"So much about Hollywood relationships is phony and contrived," Strone said. "But there was nothing fake about the way they interacted. She would touch his arm, and you could tell that there was really something there. It was completely natural; the affection between them was palpable. It was the real deal—a real love affair."

As moved as he was by the strength of their bond, Strone was equally impressed by how focused both Reeves were. "It was like any other serious business meeting, and Chris was in complete control of it," Strone said. "He asked very specific questions, and while Dana would contribute something now and then, he was in charge."

Neither gave the impression that just a couple of months earlier their lives had been turned upside down. "Here was this man who was still learning to cope with his complete inability to move," Strone said, "but after about one minute you forgot that completely. Neither one of them complained once, or showed any sign of bitterness or unhappiness at all. Both were incredibly poised."

Strone, like everyone else who encountered them around this

time, gave Dana much of the credit. "I would never even hear any tension in her voice," he said. Once or twice in Strone's presence, Chris began to have difficulty breathing. "Dana never panicked. People could be running around, but she was unflappable. I never saw her crack—not once."

Yet she "needed him as much as he needed her," Strone observed. "There was a balance in their relationship that kept them both grounded. They lived for each other—and they lived for Will."

That meeting at Kessler proved productive. Chris quickly signed with Strone, who went on to broker a $4.25 million deal with Random House for Reeve's memoirs. As he worked on the book over a two-year period, dictating it to an assistant, Chris periodically spoke with his literary agent. At social functions, Dana in particular would seek Strone out. "Dana was always positive and upbeat, no matter what horrors were going on that she and Chris had to deal with," Strone said. "She was simply the warmest, nicest, most generous, most *decent* person I've ever met."

Yet Dana had her moments. Such as when the *National Enquirer* ran a front-page story the first week in September 1995 proclaiming that Chris wanted to end his life. Under the headline "Christopher Reeve begs wife: PULL THE PLUG," the story quoted Chris as pleading with Dana to "end his misery." The tabloid went on to say that Dana had actually agreed to turn off the respirator, once she'd discovered how it could be done legally.

"You can't let them get away with that, Chris," Dana told him. "The kids are going to see this, and you don't want them thinking it's true." Together, they composed a letter to the *National Enquirer* denying the story and demanding a retraction. Just to make sure it saw the light of day, Dana passed a copy on to their friend, the nationally syndicated columnist Liz Smith.

"This article was so hurtful and so completely without foundation that I felt I had to respond," Chris wrote. "For myself, my friends and the thousands of people around the world who have expressed their love and support, I want to clearly state that your article could not be further from the truth . . . I want to live! I have not given up. I will never give up . . . An article such as yours, while distressing in the extreme, will not deter me."

By this time, Chris's initial attitude upon arriving at Kessler—a blend of fear and denial—had given way to grudging acceptance. At first, he had simply spurned all efforts to get him to read up on his injuries. Again, Dana stepped forward, this time aided by a particularly insistent nurse named Patty. "Look, Toph," she said, using that favorite pet name, "if you're going to get better—and you will—you've got to become an expert. I mean, it's *your* body."

So he carefully studied the impact his kind of spinal injury had on everything from his bowels to his breathing to his sexual function. Then he began to chip away at the wall of celebrity that stood between him and other patients at Kessler. He asked Kessler to dispense with his security guards, and soon other patients were wheeling into his room to share their stories with him—and vice versa.

Again, Dana had been instrumental in this change of heart. From the beginning, she had poked her head into other patients' rooms to see how they were doing. Then she carried their stories—along with their fond regards—back to her husband. Once he began visiting them himself, he came to the belated realization that "we were no different from one another. Some very nice friendships developed." (From this point on, Chris refused to see *Above Suspicion,* the film in which he played a paralyzed cop, because it reminded him of his own callous indifference toward the disabled. "I'm very ashamed," he later admitted, "about my smugness, my complacency. I never realized for a second that that could be me.")

Once he faced the reality of his situation, Chris attacked his disability the way he would any other adversary—with the full intention of winning. In the long run, that meant one day finding a way to reconnect and regenerate the damaged nerves in his spinal column, enabling him to walk. In the short term, it meant maintaining muscle and skin tone, slowly regaining the sensation and perhaps even movement in his upper body, and weaning himself off the ventilator.

Toward that end, Kessler's medical director, Dr. Marcalee Sipski, had Chris as her sole patient. "If I can't cure Christopher—and nobody has a cure for spinal-cord injury," she said at the time, "then my goal is to help him attain the highest quality of life he can." In Chris, she believed she had "the ideal patient—motivated and extremely sensitive to what's going on. When the doctors or therapists give him a task, you know he's going to make sure he does it perfectly. If there's an obstacle to overcome, he's going to overcome it."

Sipski's colleague, Dr. Steven Kirshblum, was the director of the Spinal Cord Unit at Kessler, and would eventually take over as Chris's principal doctor—and in the process become a close friend. He shared Sipski's belief that Chris was "very demanding on himself—more than anybody else. He set his goals very high, but the wonderful thing was that he could become joyful when he reached a goal. He'd push himself, but once he achieved something, he'd sit back and say, 'Gee, I really did accomplish something.' A lot of patients never allow themselves to enjoy these small victories."

Kirshblum was also "amazed" by the Reeves' "total lack of pretense." Unlike other celebrities the staff at Kessler had had to deal with over the years, "there was no air of VIP status about either of them," Kirshblum said, echoing the sentiment of the doctors and nurses who treated Chris at the University of Virginia Medical Center. "From the beginning, it was really 'Let's get down to business. What can we do to get Chris moving again?'"

Kirshblum, meanwhile, came in for some good-natured ribbing from his star patient; Chris often took pleasure in zeroing in on the doctor's tendency to slouch. "Out of respect for those of us who can't stand," Chris would say when Kirshblum walked into the room, "the least you can do is stand up straight!" Chris's therapist, Erica Druin, remembered how Kirshblum "threw back his shoulders every time Chris kidded him. It got to be sort of their routine. We all got a kick out of it."

In addition to helping Chris make the important medical decisions and caring for their son, Dana also had to handle both the press and the seemingly perpetual avalanche of mail from well-wishers. "Dana had to triage this," Kirshblum said. "She was literally his voice in talking to the media. Yet she remained calm, charming—I never saw her flustered."

Chris's old buddy Ken Regan was impressed by Dana's abiding sense of calm. Soon after they arrived at Kessler, she told Regan to drop by and to be sure and bring his cameras. "I'm glad she did," said Regan, who went on to chronicle Chris's battle against the

effects of paralysis on film. "Because if I wasn't looking through
a camera lens and doing my job, I think I would have lost it altogether."

Chris had always valued Dana's opinion, but now they were
truly equals in a way that they had never been before. "Dana
went," longtime friend Peter Kiernan observed, "from being a
junior partner to a full partner."

"It was testimony to the mutual respect they had for each
other," Dr. Kirshblum said. "It was the collective nature of their
relationship that I found eye-opening—the teamwork. The way
they bounced ideas off each other, it was a joy to watch—almost
thrilling. It was like watching a well-oiled machine."

Under the guidance of Dr. Sipski and then Dr. Kirshblum,
Chris would begin a demanding daily regimen that he would follow, to a large extent, for the rest of his life. It began shortly after he got up at 7:30 A.M. A nurse and a therapist would "range"
Chris's arms and legs, stretching and rotating to promote circulation. After he was dressed in sweatpants and a T-shirt, Chris was
shifted to his Quickie P-300 and rolled into the cavernous physical therapy room. The entire process thus far took no fewer than
two and a half hours.

Moved again—this time from his wheelchair to a padded exercise table—Chris went through more ranging. His arms and
legs didn't always cooperate. "The nurse is fighting to hold the
knee down and the foot up," Chris observed, "then he'll bring
it back to the middle and fight to bring my knee up to my chest.
My whole leg is fighting, the foot flapping . . . It's like watching
someone else's body—like it has nothing to do with me."

After ranging came physical therapy using a Regis Cycle, a stationary bicycle hooked up to a pair of shorts wired with electrodes. Once Chris, wearing the shorts with the electrodes attached to his thighs, quads, and calf muscles, was placed on the Regis Cycle, a 50-volt electric current would stimulate the muscles. Those muscles, in turn, would push the pedals. This $100,000 bike, along with a similar device called the StimMaster ($30,000) that could also be used to work the arms and stomach muscles, enabled Chris to maintain a surprising degree of muscle tone.

Chris then spent more time doing more neck exercises, shoulder shrugs, and chin tucks—a minimum of fifty repetitions each. Then came a full hour of occupational therapy—learning, for example, the finer points of his Quickie model wheelchair and a similar sip-and-puff control panel that operated his lights, fan, and television. He learned how to coordinate his speech with the respirator, so that he could start his sentence on the outward breath and continue at least a word or two of the next thought so that the listener understood that he was not yet finished. Chris also learned about the voice-activated telephone and computer that would eventually be installed at his home.

After he went through the daily routine of being "coughed"— having a nurse use a vacuumlike coughalator to suction the mucus that built up in his throat and lungs—Chris would be visited in the afternoon by a respiratory therapist. They would spend the next hour or more working on Chris's breathing exercises. To measure his capacity, the trach tube was closed off and Chris was left to take in as much air as he could on his own and then breathe it out. To be weaned off the ventilator, Chris would have to take in over 1,000 cc's of air. Even after months of training at

Kessler, he could only manage to pull in 75 cc's of air on his own—roughly the lung capacity of a canary.

Dana watched as her husband struggled for every breath, and saw the frustration on his face when he failed to make significant progress. "It takes time, honey," she reassured him. "You'll get there. You'll get there." Chris had begun calling Dr. Sipski "Coach," but it was a moniker that might better have been applied to Dana. Always at his elbow offering hugs, laughter, and words of encouragement, she made a vow "not to let Chris get depressed. He's incredibly positive," she said, "and not a defeatist by any means. But there are times when we all feel that we've just had it, you know? Sometimes you've got to be reminded that there's light at the end of the tunnel."

Dana got some help in this endeavor from Kessler's director of psychology Dr. Craig Alexander, who met with Chris frequently to help him deal with the ever-present emotional hurdles. But nothing lifted his spirits more than the few minutes he spent each day practically standing on his own two feet. Chris would be placed flat on his back on a tilt table and strapped in securely before one of the ends was gradually cranked up. The first few times he was brought to a near-upright position, Chris's blood pressure plummeted and he passed out. But after several practice runs, he was able to be brought up to an eighty-degree angle—for all intents and purposes as if he were standing on his own legs.

Even though she was on hand during these initial attempts using the tilt table, Dana was moved by the sight of all six-feet-four inches of Chris "standing." The first time she looked up at him, she began crying, and had to leave the room. Later, she got in the habit of standing on the footrests of the table alongside him, and putting her head on his shoulder—"Just like the old days," he told her.

No less a battle-hardened veteran of the spinal injury wars than Dr. Sipski also marveled at the sight. "I was used to looking down at him," she said. "For the first time, I had to look up. He's really tall and has these huge, piercing, blue eyes. He looked like what I was used to seeing in the movies."

Soon, Dana brought Will in to see Daddy on the tilt table. The little boy walked in the door of the physical therapy gym and only managed a few steps before stopping. He gazed up at his father as if he were looking at the angel on top of a Christmas tree. "Wow!" he said. "You're really *big*!" Then, with Dana cheering him on, Will ran up and hugged one of Daddy's legs.

From that point on, whenever Chris was on the tilt table, Dana and Will climbed aboard and joined him in a group hug. Will, who had become used to clambering over his father's wheelchair, now climbed all the way to the peak of the tilt table, pausing to enjoy the view from atop Daddy's head.

By September, Chris, with no small amount of prodding from Dana, decided it was time to step back into the spotlight—if only to set the record straight about his so-called "death wish"—and to thank the 300,000 people who had written him letters of support.

No one had been more persistent than Barbara Walters, who along with everyone else in television considered landing the first interview with Christopher Reeve to be the "get" of the year. Chris had known Barbara for a long time—she interviewed him when the first of his *Superman* films came out seventeen years earlier—and the two were fond of each other. Dana, in particular, had always been in awe of Walters. She actually made the call to Barbara telling her of their decision to give her the interview. "I couldn't believe it," Walters said, "and of course we really had no idea of what to expect. But Dana was always so upbeat and positive. She made it very clear from the beginning that they were very enthusiastic about the interview—they wanted to let people know that Chris was all right."

The Reeves' prime-time interview with Walters on ABC's *20/20* was taped at Kessler over a three-day period and aired on September 29, 1995. During the interview, Chris admitted for the first time that he had briefly considered ending it all ("I'd lie awake at night and think, *What's going to become of me?*") and described movingly how Dana's love pulled him back from the brink.

"Oh, my God! There's this commitment—true commitment," he told Walters. "Dana and I were always in love, but I would say we've now transcended into something where our moments together are even more valuable than they ever were."

Reliving the accident and the grueling months that followed, Chris betrayed not the slightest hint of bitterness. And he spoke optimistically about his prospects for recovery, predicting that he would be walking again within the decade.

"You begin to see there is a future," he said. "And that the love and support and friendship of family and friends and people around the world, as all these things came to me and I realized their value . . . Am I lucky. I am so lucky."

As for his prospects of ever walking again: "I would like to stand up on my fiftieth birthday—that's seven years from now," he told Walters, "and raise a glass to everyone who helped me."

The impact of the Reeves' joint appearance on television—
one of the year's highest-rated broadcasts—was immediate.
Overnight, Chris was being hailed as an inspiration not just for
victims of spinal cord injuries but for disabled people everywhere.
Not long after, he was interviewed by the *Today* show's Katie
Couric, who devoted an entire week to exploring the subject of
spinal cord injuries.

It was clearly time, Dana believed, for Chris to rejoin the world.
She reminded him that on October 17, the Creative Coalition that
he helped found was having its annual fundraising dinner at New
York's Pierre Hotel. His close friend Robin Williams was being
honored by the group that night for his Comic Relief concerts
with Whoopi Goldberg and Billy Crystal that had raised millions
for the homeless.

"It would be wonderful if you could present that award to
Robin yourself," Dana told him. "Wouldn't it be great to see your
old friends? They'll all be there."

There were risks, to be sure. His body could go into violent
spasms at any time. He might become detached from the vent and
suddenly be gasping for breath, or suffer a bout of dysreflexia—a
life-threatening condition brought about suddenly and silently by
an obstructed urinary tract, bowel, or catheter. That obstruction
can cause a sharp spike in blood pressure, leading in turn to a coro-
nary or a stroke. What if, gripped by stage fright, he simply forgot how to speak while on the ventilator? What if the leg bag into
which his urine emptied began leaking or simply broke?

Chris and Dana talked over each and every possible calamity, but
in the end she convinced him that this was the perfect opportunity to show the world that he was back—and to publicly thank

his loyal friend in the process. "Besides," Dana said, "Robin will be out there on the stage with you. So what have you got to worry about?"

"That's precisely why I *am* worried," Chris shot back.

Dana took charge once again, ordering a special van to take them into Manhattan, arranging for Juice and a Kessler nurse to come along, even rummaging through Chris's closet in Bedford to find his favorite black tuxedo. Realizing that there would be a small army of reporters and photographers on hand to record Chris's first public appearance since the accident, Dana also worked with Robin's security people on a strategy to protect her husband. Rather than approach the Pierre through its main Fifth Avenue entrance, the Reeves' van pulled up to the side entrance on East 61st Street. A special canopy had already been constructed from the curb to the side door of the hotel. Within seconds of the Reeves' arrival, guards taped over the van windows so no one could see in.

No one even got a glimpse of Chris or Dana as they were spirited out of the van, beneath the canopy, and into the hotel. After resting up briefly in the bedroom of an elegant nineteenth-floor suite, Chris and Dana were escorted into the living room.

A cheer went up from more than twenty friends who were there to greet them, including Barbara Walters, Susan Sarandon, Blythe Danner, New York City mayor Rudy Giuliani and his then-wife Donna Hanover, Blair Brown, Ron Silver, Carly Simon—and Robin and Marsha Williams. "The mascara," said actress Stockard Channing, "will be runny tonight."

But for the moment, Robin Williams was determined to lighten the mood. "Better be careful using that wheelchair in New

York," Williams cracked, "panhandlers will offer to wash your wheels." Dana burst into her trademark, full-throttle laugh and clapped, and Chris laughed with her. For the next half hour, he chatted amiably with everyone. "I never knew," he told news-woman Linda Ellerbee, "how many potholes there were in New York until I went over them today. When you're in a wheelchair that's strapped in a van—let's say it changes your perspective. That, and being stuck in a hospital for five months."

"He was in great spirits," marveled Ellerbee. And so was every-body else. "It's like Christmas having Chris here," Danner said. "He's such a generous man." Concurred Carly Simon: "He's a bright light, a bright spirit. He reaches out to so many people. He's got guts and stamina and soul and strength."

No one realized that, beneath the amiable chitchat, Chris was worried about all the things that might go wrong. So were Dana, Juice, and the nurse who had forced him to read up on his condition, Patty. Working in concert, Dana distracted every-one with a story about Will's latest antics while Patty deftly checked Chris's vital signs without ever disturbing the flow of conversation.

An hour later, Chris was in the wings of the grand ballroom stage, waiting to be introduced by Susan Sarandon. Once he was announced and Juice wheeled him onstage, the seven hundred people who jammed the ballroom leaped to their feet and gave him a five-minute standing ovation.

Then Chris explained why he'd come. A former English teacher of his once told him "the only reason for nonattendance is quadruple amputation—and even then they can carry you in a basket." So, Chris told the crowd, "I thought I'd better show up."

Thrilled with the audience's response, Chris went on to introduce Glenn "Juice" Miller ("He used to lead a band") and then Dana. When he thanked her for saving him—"I owe her my life"—the crowd burst into sustained applause again. Pausing periodically to catch his next breath from the ventilator, Chris acknowledged that he "never knew there was such love and support aimed in my direction. Thank you from the bottom of my heart."

By the time Robin Williams took to the stage to receive his award from Chris, half the audience was weeping. Williams quickly put an end to that. He admitted that he visited Chris's room in the guise of "a Russian proctologist—the results were good," and then launched into a fifteen-minute routine with Chris as his straight man. Among other things, Robin suggested his friend enter a tractor pull, and volunteered to auction off Chris's snazzy new "tie"—his ventilator tube—for charity.

Then, eying his wheelchair, Robin praised his friend. "You're on a roll, bro," he said. "Literally."

Back in his room at Kessler that night, Chris and Dana were giddy. The evening, which had seemed so terrifying at first, marked a new beginning—and not just for Chris. "People saw that Dana was the main reason Chris had gotten through this," Dr. Kirshblum said. "More and more people were seeing what an exceptional woman she was."

Using Dixie cups Dana had purloined from the nurses' station, the Reeves toasted what she jokingly referred to as Chris's "triumphant return to the stage" with white wine. "You loved it, didn't you?" she teased. "All the attention—and the applause. I was watching you the whole time, Toph, and you just loved it."

"You know me," he replied wryly, "too well."

From that night on, Chris and Dana began seriously planning Chris's homecoming—and what he intended to do with the rest of his life. Before the accident, he had been set to direct a film. Even those who doubted that Chris would ever walk again, like Dr. Marcalee Sipski, believed that was possible. "I expect him to direct as many movies as he wants," she said. "I don't see any barriers in his way."

Perhaps. But Chris wanted more. He was determined to walk again, and knew that the barriers yet to be overcome for that to ever happen were monumental. Dana had done everything she could to keep Chris from sinking into depression, including plastering the walls of his room at Kessler with notes and cards from countless well-wishers—as well as the NASA poster signed by every current astronaut. "This is what it's going to take to make that happen, Toph," she said, pointing to the poster. "Another effort like the space program."

Reaching the moon was one thing, but marshaling the kind of support—and cash—that would be needed for research to "cure" spinal cord injuries by regenerating cells was quite another. At Kessler, Chris was visited by some of the leading experts and activists in the field—most notably by pioneer researcher Dr. Wise Young of New York University–Bellevue Medical Center and Henry Steifel, chairman of the American Paralysis Association.

What was needed, they all agreed, was a recognizable face to put on the problem—someone to lead the fight. "What they need," Dana told Chris, "is Superman."

Whatever his other achievements on screen, Chris realized full well that the moviegoing public—not just here but around the world—identified him as the Man of Steel. "Not a bad thing,

Toph," Dana reminded him, "to be loved by millions of people for being a superhero." She also pointed out that he had a friend in the White House; Chris had campaigned actively for Bill Clinton in 1992, and the two men had spoken on the phone several times since the accident. Over the years, the Reeves had also forged friendships with several senators and congressmen as they crusaded on behalf of the National Endowment for the Humanities and the environment.

"Maybe I can do something, Dana," he said. "Maybe this is the one way I can make sense of all this." Chris picked up the gauntlet at the American Paralysis Association's annual fund-raising dinner at New York's Waldorf Astoria Hotel in early November. Not only did he prevail upon his pal Paul Newman to host the event, but he gave the keynote speech. Its theme drew on the parallels Dana saw between JFK's pledge to put a man on the moon and efforts to treat paralysis. "This time," Chris declared, "our mission is the conquest of *inner space*—the brain and central nervous system."

Just so there was no doubt about what his personal goals were, Chris reiterated his desire to be walking by age fifty. "That's just seven years from now," he quipped, "so we better get cracking."

The evening brought in $985,000—more than three times the record for any previous APA fund-raiser. By the end of the month, Chris was asked to join the organization's board of directors—as its chairman.

Before agreeing to take on this daunting new responsibility, Chris talked it over with Dana. "Do I really want to be the poster boy for spinal cord injuries?" he asked her bluntly. "I've got you and the kids to think of."

She reassured him that she and the children would be fine with whatever he chose to do. But Dana also made it clear where she stood on the issue. After reeling off the names of several of the patients he had befriended at Kessler, she asked if he thought he could really make a difference in any of their lives. "I think you can," she told him. "But of course it's all up to you."

In truth, it had taken Dana a considerable amount of time and effort to get Chris to this place. "Dana was the daughter of a physician," Dr. Kirshblum said. "She saw the handwriting on the wall early on. She never babied him or treated him as disabled, but she tried to make it as easy as possible for him to come to terms with his new reality. Her mind-set allowed her to see the bigger picture, even before he did."

"Dana saw around the corner first," agreed Peter Kiernan. "She thought, *All I have to do is kick the can down the road a little bit before we face the long road ahead.* Dana lovingly guided Chris to this place." Added Kirshblum: "The overarching feeling was that he was going to make his mark in a bigger way—that he had something to do beyond moving his hands or legs. She realized far earlier than he did what their role would be in the world. That is why she didn't crack."

Chris accepted the challenge. In the coming weeks he studied not only the specifics of his own particular injury, but everything he could get his hands on regarding the broad spectrum of spinal cord research. He was stunned to learn that $8.7 billion was being spent each year just to keep spinal cord injury victims alive, and that by adding a meager $40 million per year to research, scientists believed they could make significant progress.

In much the same way polio victim FDR launched the government war on polio in the 1940s that eventually led to a vaccine, Chris could lead the fight for ways to repair spinal cord injuries. There would be a huge difference in their approaches: While Roosevelt was rarely photographed in his wheelchair, Chris would seek to raise public awareness by never concealing his condition from the public.

First, however, there were more obstacles to overcome. Not content to be totally dependent on the ventilator, Chris managed in a matter of three days—with Dana in the wings cheering him on—to raise the output of his lungs tenfold. Soon he would be able to breathe on his own for as long as half an hour.

Delighted with his progress, Chris's doctors gave him permission to spend Thanksgiving with his family in Bedford. On the ride up from New Jersey with Chuck, one of Reeve's favorite aides, Chris and Dana chatted excitedly about who would be there, what Will was up to, and simply how great it was to see the old homestead.

As the van pulled up the long, fence-lined driveway to his house, however, Chris suddenly became emotional. While the rest of the family waited to greet them at the front door, Dana and Chris remained in the van for twenty minutes; she held him in her arms as they both wept. "It's OK," she said, trying to comfort him. "It's OK. You're home now. You're finally home."

"There was a Rip Van Winkle effect," Chris later said of that moment. "I had been away for so long, and here I was, home again, but under very different circumstances. I couldn't even walk up the steps . . . Things would never be the same."

Once they pulled themselves together, Chris and Dana were

warmly greeted by a dozen Reeves and Morosinis. But this home-coming was far from joyful. Because the house had yet to be out-fitted with ramps and wider doorways, Chris spent most of the day trapped in the living room. He did not like having to ask family members to help every time he needed something, and when it came time to eat, he felt self-conscious about having to be liter-ally spoon-fed turkey and mashed potatoes by his wife.

There was one moment, however, that made the visit worth-while. It had always been a Reeve family tradition to go around the table and have each person talk about the things that person was most thankful for. Out of deference to Chris, no one men-tioned that they were thankful for their good health. Instead, they spoke about how grateful they were for their spouses and their chil-dren. To this, Chris and Dana added their gratitude for the doc-tors, staff, and the patients at Kessler, and the thousands of strangers who had written letters of support. Will topped them all. When asked what he was most grateful for, he answered with a single word: "Dad."

Nevertheless, Chris was angry and depressed when he was loaded back into his van at five-thirty for the trip back to Kessler. He wanted to stay overnight, but his insurance company refused to allow it—unless, of course, he wanted to absorb the $1,300 per day cost himself.

Not surprisingly, the cost to the Reeves of caring for Chris would prove to be nothing less than staggering. First, Dana had to make sure that both their Bedford home and the house in Williamstown were outfitted with special ramps, and that door-ways were widened for wheelchair access.

Making these changes *inside* their sprawling Bedford home was

one thing. But when Dana said she wanted to install a ramp leading up to their front door, Chris refused. "No way," he said. "I
don't want it to look like a disabled person lives here!"

Dana cocked her head. "Hello?" she replied. "A disabled person *does* live here!"

The argument dragged on for weeks. "I wouldn't back down
on that one, and he was just as stubborn," she remembered.
"I think it was the final thing of Chris admitting that he was
disabled."

Finally, Dana showed Chris a plan for the ramp that he could
accept—a gently sloping incline made of slate and lined with
flower boxes. When he finally saw how the finished project actually enhanced the exterior of the house, Chris gushed, "Oh,
it's gorgeous!"

Renovating the house was only half the equation. Dana also put
herself in charge of hiring home-care nurses, as well as aides to lift
Chris out of bed and into his wheelchair—and vice versa. Not that
she wasn't capable of handling much of the job on her own. "Dana
learned everything those nurses do," said Barbara Walters. "She
knows how to move him, to change him—she can do everything
now." Another friend, longtime New Jersey Shakespeare Festival
director Bonnie Monte, agreed that Chris was "so lucky to have
her"—although Monte conceded that Dana routinely joked
"about the media portraying her as 'St. Dana.' But she doesn't want
to be that. She says, 'I am just a woman whose husband fell off a
horse, and I'm going to take care of him. That's what you do.'"

Still, Chris and Dana made a decision that would turn out to
be the key to sustaining their marriage. "I can't be your nurse and
I won't be your mother," Dana said. "If this is going to work, I

have got to be just one thing: your wife." It was a valuable piece of advice Chris had already received from Craig Alexander and other psychologists at Kessler; too many marriages had collapsed under the stress of having one partner bear all the caretaking responsibilities.

"I could easily see how this could break up a rocky marriage," Dana later told her friend Liz Smith. "You'd say, 'Forget it. I can't take it.' Because it's a burden. There a lot about this that's a burden."

At times, friends and colleagues seemed to forget just how much of the burden Dana shouldered. "As a caretaker she was unbelievable," Chris's literary agent Dan Strone said. "People would always walk up to Dana and the first thing they would ask is 'How's Chris?' They might then ask about how Dana was feeling, but you got the sense that her welfare was always secondary. That must have been hard on her."

Yet from the beginning, Chris pointed out, "Dana never flinched from our commitment—not once . . . When you have an accident like this, it magnifies your situation. If you had a bad marriage before, it's going to get worse. If you have a wonderful marriage, it's going to get even better."

The person who was most surprised by Dana's strength was Dana herself. "Chris is ten years older than me and in subtle ways *he* took care of *me*," she mused. When he was hospitalized, Dana said, "suddenly I was in charge. He's still my mentor in many ways, but what's nice is I grew up in his eyes, too. I became his equal in a more profound way than ever before. Now he comes to me for advice as much as I go to him. It's created a stronger partnership and deepened the bond between us."

As much as he depended on Dana's love, support, and, frequently, her growing expertise as a caretaker, Chris was determined that she not give her life solely over to him. "It's already been so trying for Dana," he told a former Juilliard classmate. "She's had to give up so much . . . I want her to have a career, to have her own life. She's terrific, but she's a human being. I don't want her resenting me."

One of the burdens they both had to face was the sheer cost of keeping Chris alive—more than $400,000 annually (it would soon rise to over $550,000 per year). With a lifetime cap on his insurance of $1.2 million, it looked at the time as if Chris's insurance would run out in three years. And because of his spinal cord injury, he would be prevented from obtaining insurance elsewhere. Dana had one word to describe the prospect of having to somehow bear the cost of caring for Chris: "Terrifying."

A possible solution, not only for the Reeves but for every American facing a catastrophic illness, was offered by Vermont senator James Jeffords. The senator wanted to add an amendment to the Kennedy-Kassebaum health bill that would require insurance companies to raise the lifetime cap from $1 million to $10 million. When Jeffords called asking if he would support the measure, Chris promptly dictated a letter to every senator urging them to pass the amendment. (It was narrowly defeated a month later.)

In the meantime, Chris, who had earned millions as an actor, would have to go to work to make sure his medical bills didn't force his family into bankruptcy. The $4.25 million book deal with Random House was an important first step in the right direction, but Dana still looked ahead to a financial future that to her seemed nothing short of "scary."

On December 15, 1995, Chris and Dana finally left Kessler and moved home to Bedford to begin their new life with Will. Once again, Chris became so emotional as they pulled up to the house that he had to pause with Dana in the car for a few moments before gathering up the courage to go inside.

Since the house had yet to be modified, Chris knew he would be restricted to the ground floor; the dining room was turned into his bedroom, with a single bed alongside for Dana to sleep on. However, Chris found the difficulty of even moving from one room to the next irksome. "There were steps up to the dining room and down to the living room, and thresholds everywhere," he later said. "I couldn't move ten feet without it being a big production. I always feel like I'm putting people out, so naturally I spent the first few weeks more or less constantly apologizing."

Williamstown was altogether different. Since the renovations had already been finished, Chris could use his sip-and-puff wheelchair to move around the house relatively unencumbered. As he had done at Kessler, Will often climbed on his dad's lap and urged him on as they careened down hallways and across rooms in Chris's Quickie P300. "He treats it," Chris told Dana, "like his personal go-cart." Nor was Will reluctant to burst into their temporary bedroom any time of the day or night. At five-thirty one morning, he burst through the doors and flapped his arms furiously as he spun around the room. "Look!" said the three-year-old. "I'm a hummingbird!"

When family and friends came to visit the Reeves in Bedford, they were surprised to find how smoothly things ran—thanks to Dana. "Dana was a believer in routine and structure," her older sister, Deborah, said. Conversely, Dana's younger sister, Adrienne, was "surprised by how happy the house was" even in the weeks immediately following his return from Kessler. "It still had that same busyness and a lot of laughter."

Still, being home only reminded Chris that, at least as far as frolicking outside with the rest of the family was concerned, his role was now strictly that of spectator. While Dana, Will, Matthew, and Alex tossed snowballs at one another, Dad watched from one of the house's expansive windows.

There were practical reasons for Chris not to venture outdoors; no fewer than nineteen snowstorms slammed into the Northeast that winter, making it treacherous for even able-bodied people to get around. Then there was the sheer magnitude of the undertaking. Every time Chris wanted to leave the house, it required hours of preparation and the efforts of up to a half dozen people. Once he arrived at his destination—a restaurant or a theater, for example—there were usually additional obstacles.

"There is nothing that is easy," Dana said. "Everything is a struggle. And of course we are mourning the loss of Chris's mobility and moving on from that . . ." To safeguard her husband from potential embarrassment, Dana now called ahead before every family outing to make sure there was wheelchair access. On many occasions, she also carried a small portable ramp with her—just in case someone forgot to mention a step or a curb.

"Every time Chris is reminded of his disability, it's depressing for him," Dana said. "I don't want him to have to say, 'It's too much trouble, let's go home. I hate this.'" Regardless of Dana's efforts, there were such times when Chris felt the pitying eyes of others, and he grew increasingly reluctant to leave the comfort and security of home.

As wary as he was of being seen in public, Chris was determined to resume his role in Will's life. Just three weeks after Chris left Kessler, Will was sitting on Dad's lap at New York's Big Apple Circus, wearing a red clown nose and watching the animals and acrobats. Dana, said another spectator, "could not take her eyes off Will or her hands off her husband. She was obviously just so delighted to be there as a family."

As it happened, that visit underscored just how fragile Chris still was. A few days after the trip to the circus, Chris woke up with a crippling headache. He knew this feeling all too well; it was a sign of life-threatening dysreflexia caused by a urinary tract or bowel obstruction. When the nurse confirmed that his blood pressure had skyrocketed, Chris turned to Dana. "Get me to the hospital," he told her, "*now*."

Dana dialed 911, and within minutes an ambulance was speeding Chris to Northern Westchester Hospital. After he was treated for dysreflexia—this time the blockage was the result of an impacted colon—Chris was released, only to discover that he had now contracted a blood infection.

As far as Chris was concerned, these setbacks validated his fear of the outside world. He had not given up on rejoining society, but, for the time being, he would focus on his own health. Mornings were set aside for exercise, physical therapy, and breathing lessons (he would soon be able to spend up to ninety minutes at a time off the ventilator)—and doing whatever he could to raise awareness and money for spinal cord research. That, and continuing to lobby lawmakers on behalf of insurance reform.

The software engineers at AM Technologies in Newtown, Massachusetts, made things a lot easier for Chris when they presented him with a customized version of the voice-activated computer program Dragon Dictate. With it, Chris could operate the computer, fax, and phone. In addition to sending e-mail, he could talk with Matthew and Alexandra in England and could even play long-distance chess with Matthew.

Chris could also communicate with his accountants and lawyers as he and Dana made tough decisions about their personal finances. One such decision was to sell off a number of assets, including Eastern Express—the horse Chris still affectionately called "Buck." The asking price for Buck: $25,000.

The decision to sell Eastern Express was strictly a financial one; Chris made it abundantly clear in all his interviews and public statements that he held no animosity whatsoever toward Buck. In fact, both he and Dana felt sorry for the animal that would forever be known as the horse that maimed Superman. "He's a beautiful, sweet-natured animal," Chris said. "None of what happened was his fault. Something spooked him, that's all. It happens. I'm hoping he'll have a long and happy life with his new owners. He's a wonderful horse."

For nearly ten months following the accident in Culpeper, Chris had Buck boarded at Gathering Farm in Hamilton, Massachusetts. He not only phoned the stables regularly to check on Buck's welfare, but he had videos of the horse's workout sessions sent to him so he could review Buck's progress.

Dana understood Chris's need to keep Buck for a time—the horse was an important link to Chris's past as an accomplished horseman—and not to succumb to feelings of resentment toward the animal that paralyzed him. "Everyone acts surprised that I don't hate Buck for doing this to my husband," Dana confided to a friend. "Someone told me, 'I would have just gotten a gun and shot him.' But if Chris doesn't feel anger toward Buck, how can I?"

That sentiment so moved influential Orange County horse-woman and philanthropist Joan Irvine Smith that she donated $1 million for the establishment of the Reeve-Irvine Center for spinal cord research at the University of California at Irvine. Then she prodded the State of California to match her dollar for dollar. The East Coast–oriented Chris, who had been unfamil-iar with Smith and had to be persuaded that UC-Irvine was a prestigious university campus, marveled at Smith's ability to get things done. "Joan is the kind of woman," he conceded, "you want on your side."

For all his successes on the home front, Chris was now suf-fering from a kind of agoraphobia—with each passing day, he grew more and more dependent on the safe, insular worlds he had created for himself at Bedford and Williamstown. Dana made repeated overtures to get him out and about—to dinner or to see a movie—but to no avail. "I know the kind of man he is," Dana told one of Chris's aides. "He's a very social, outgoing guy. He hates being cooped up, and I hate to see him giving in to this fear. I wish there was a way to break him of this . . ."

Dana's prayers were answered when producer Quincy Jones called Chris up in early February and invited him to appear at the sixty-eighth annual Academy Awards ceremonies to be held on March 25. Listening to Jones over the speakerphone, Chris could scarcely believe what he was hearing. The same Holly-wood movers and shakers who he thought had all but written him off now embraced him as one of their own.

Chris suggested that he might use the opportunity to talk about the power of films not just to entertain, but to have real social impact. Yet, when they were finished hashing over ideas, Jones realized that he still did not have a definite answer from Chris. "So you want to think about it?" he asked tentatively.

"I'm very honored by the invitation, Quincy," Chris answered. "So let me think about it . . ." Then, before ending the call, Chris blurted out his answer. "You know what, I'll do it."

Sitting in the kitchen, Dana could hear every word of the conversation. She was thrilled at the idea, but knew it was a decision Chris had to make for himself. When Jones hung up, she could hear Chris say to himself, "What have I done?"

Chris then wheeled himself into the kitchen to tell Dana about the conversation. Before he could finish, she interrupted him. "Do it," Dana said, looking straight into his eyes. "Do it."

Over the next few weeks, Jones learned just how focused Chris could be. He wanted to illustrate his "Hollywood Tackles the Issues" speech with clips from such groundbreaking films as *Platoon, Philadelphia,* and *Norma Rae.* "People think of people in wheelchairs as helpless geeks," Chris told Jones. "I want them to see someone who is still strong in spite of being paralyzed."

Toward that end, he insisted that the montage of clips shown during his appearance include Jon Voight in his Oscar-winning performance as the wheelchair-bound Vietnam vet who falls in love with Jane Fonda in *Coming Home.* Among other things, the film gave moviegoers an eye-opening lesson in wheelchair sex.

Chris's Oscar surprise was carried out with all the precision of a secret military campaign. "I've worked on a lot of projects, including a presidential inauguration," Oscar coproducer David

Saltzman recalled, "but nothing compares with getting Christopher to the Oscars."

Planning began in February, when Neil Stutzer, whose firm coordinated travel for people with disabilities, began assembling a team that would make Chris's three-day visit to Hollywood possible. Stutzer pored over floor plans at the Dorothy Chandler Pavilion and discussed everything from the deployment of security guards to on-site emergency medical facilities with top Academy officials. The result: a seventy-five-page manual that even included how to go about repairing Chris's wheelchair if it broke down.

In the meantime, Chris had other duties to attend to. He went on *Larry King Live* to make a direct appeal for donations to the American Paralysis Association. Then, on March 18, he flew to Green Springs, Ohio, to christen an $18 million wing of the St. Francis Health Care Center. "I'm glad to be here," he told patients at the center. "Actually, I'm glad to be anywhere!" The ice broken, Chris then went on to credit Dana with saving his life. "She was there, standing off to the side, smiling shyly," said one patient. "You can see the support that he gets from her. She is his backbone."

On March 23, the Reeves began their Oscar odyssey. By this time, Chris had come close to backing out three times—only to have Dana talk him back into going through with it. Quincy Jones, meanwhile, had asked Warner Bros. to fly Chris, Dana, and their entourage of doctors, nurses, and aides to Los Angeles aboard a corporate jet. Chris was loaded onto the plane on a stretcher—being prone would limit any physical damage if the plane hit unexpected turbulence—and the assembled medical team constantly monitored his vital signs as they jetted across the continent.

Once on the ground in L.A., the Reeve party departed the jet in a specially outfitted van with blacked-out windows and were driven directly to the Beverly Hilton, where Chris and Dana were registered under an assumed name. They entered the hotel through the garage, boarded an express elevator to their floor, and, with hotel personnel making sure the coast was clear, made their way to their suite undetected.

That Oscar night eve, the Reeves dined with their pals Robin and Marsha Williams in their room, and then hosted friends like Chris's *Remains of the Day* costar Emma Thompson and Alec Baldwin in the hotel's presidential suite. The next day, L.A. radio stations began to leak the news that Chris would make a surprise appearance at the Oscars. Nevertheless, the secrecy continued. Chris attended closed-set rehearsals, then was spirited back to the hotel for an hour-long nap. He then got dressed in formal wear for the evening—a two-and-a-half-hour-long process.

With Dana at his side, Chris returned to the Dorothy Chandler Pavilion around 6 P.M., and watched the show from his dressing room. As it unfolded before a global audience of more than two billion, the show would turn out to be even more fraught with emotion than usual. Early on, actor Paul Sorvino openly wept as his daughter Mira accepted her Best Supporting Actress award for *Mighty Aphrodite.* The tears continued to flow as Kirk Douglas, still severely speech-impaired after a devastating stroke, accepted a life achievement award while his four wet-eyed sons looked on. Later the camera focused on the anguished faces of audience members as Gerda Weissmann Klein, who was profiled in the best documentary short subject, told movingly of her experiences during the Holocaust.

As the evening built to the inevitable crescendo he would supply, Chris was all business. He insisted that he be wheeled into position center stage *before* his introduction ("I don't want people to see me being pushed onstage") and, with only twenty minutes to spare, told Quincy Jones that he did not want to be introduced to the theme music from *Superman*. Jones and the orchestra, which had already rehearsed the piece, searched frantically for new music.

Still having problems with his voice, Chris called Dr. Steven Kirshblum back at Kessler. "I spoke to him right before he was to go on. We talked about how we could use some techniques to get his voice a little stronger. He was *so* excited."

Keenly aware that there was no time delay—that whatever happened would be seen live—Chris still worried that his wheelchair might hit a bump and cause him to spasm uncontrollably. "If you spasm," his doctor had told him, "it's only human—it'll make people aware of what can happen to spinal cord victims." But Chris did not want to become the object of pity.

As he was wheeled out of his dressing room, Chris did hit a threshold. The bump caused him to flop over at the waist and his arms and legs were left hanging. Dana and the aides scrambled to reposition him.

Unaware of what was going on backstage, the unseen announcer intoned, "Ladies and Gentleman, Christopher Reeve"— and the curtain rose to reveal Chris alone center stage in his wheelchair.

Dana stood in the wings with Chris's doctor and nurses, anxious about the possibility that something might go wrong but, more than anything, thrilled about the reception that awaited her husband. "I am just so proud of him," she whispered to one of Chris's aides as the curtain went up. "So proud."

Instantly, the entire star-packed audience of three thousand rose to its feet. Dana and the rest of Chris's team, watching from the sidelines, were all crying with joy. "Everybody was bawling," said one of Chris's nurses. "Big stars, stagehands, musicians—everybody."

Chris gazed out at some of the most famous people in the world. "I saw so many warm and accepting faces," he later said. "It felt like a homecoming."

Chris drank it all in before beginning. "What you probably don't know," he said with a wry smile, "is that I left New York last September and I just arrived here this morning." He went on, "And I'm glad I did, because I wouldn't have missed this kind of welcome for the world."

Then he launched into his message for the evening: that movies can, do, and should make a difference. "When I was a kid, my friends and I went to the movies just for fun," he said. "But then we saw Stanley Kubrick's *Dr. Strangelove,* which started us thinking about the madness of nuclear destruction. Stanley Kramer's *The Defiant Ones* taught us about race relations. It was then we began to realize films could deal with social issues." Hollywood, he went on, "needs to do more. Let's continue to take risks. Let's tackle the issues. In many ways, our film community can do it better than anyone else."

The curtain came down to more thunderous applause, and

Dana rushed to Chris's side and kissed him on the lips. "You were wonderful," she said, wiping a tear away with her hand.

Chris looked up at her and smiled broadly. "It was amazing, wasn't it?"

In a private room afterward, Dana beamed while such figures as Steven Spielberg, Tom Cruise, Nicole Kidman, and Quincy Jones toasted her husband. The Reeves then moved on to the Governor's Ball, where his old pals Robin Williams and Susan Sarandon—who happened to have picked up a Best Actress Oscar that night for *Dead Man Walking*—were among those who stopped by his table to celebrate Chris's return. Mel Gibson, who won two Academy Awards that night for *Braveheart,* echoed the sentiments of many. "The attitude he's got—he'll walk," Gibson said. "I have no doubts about it."

For the time being, Chris was willing to settle for once again being among his peers in the film industry. "Chris loved showing people," observed his agent Scott Henderson that night, "that he's back."

But what about Dana? That night at the hotel, after his nurse and two aides had spent the two-and-a-half hours it took each night to get him into bed, Chris told Dana it was time she started thinking about her own future as an actress. "You've done so much for me and the kids," he said. "But work means as much to you as it does to me."

Dana had already been offered a job—playing the part of Julia in the New Jersey Shakespeare Festival's production of *Two Gentlemen of Verona*. "It's important for you both to get back to doing what you do," the festival's director, Bonnie Monte, had told her.

The theater in New Jersey was close enough so that Dana

could commute there from home each day, and Chris felt comfortable alone in the house with the nurses and aides who now cared for him. Will's nanny was first-rate, and when Will wasn't climbing all over his dad, Chris loved to watch him cavort in the front yard.

Still, Dana worried about leaving her husband for so many hours each day. What if something went wrong and she wasn't there? Think of how scared Will would be without his mother there to reassure him.

Chris listened patiently to Dana's concerns, and when she was finished the only sound in the room was the whoosh of his ventilator. "Come here," he said with a tilt of his head, and Dana walked over so that they could look squarely into each other's eyes.

"Do it," he said firmly. "Do it."

"They just don't allow themselves
to be self-pitying. That takes an
awful lot of strength."
—*Margot Kidder,*
friend and Superman *costar*

"We are more focused on what really
matters—the family and how far love
can take you."
—*Dana*

"I realized: Man, am I lucky—
I am so lucky."
—*Chris*

"It was pretty unglamorous,
pretty darn unromantic.
But Dana was in it for the
long haul."

—*Peter Kiernan,*
close friend and chairman
of the Christopher and Dana
Reeve Foundation

"You could tell how much they loved each
other. She was going to do anything in
the world for him, and—if the situation were
reversed—he would do the same for her."

—*Brooke Ellison,*
friend

"I was married to a man who never gave up."

—*Dana*

6

A Sunday Morning
Williamstown

C hris gazes across the sun-filled living room at Dana, who sits cross-legged on the couch reading the Arts and Leisure section of the *New York Times*. He suddenly finds her little mannerisms—the way she scans the ads before lighting on an article that interests her, how she rests her coffee mug on her right knee and laughs out loud when something she reads really amuses her—arousing.

Dana looks up and realizes that this whole time he has been sitting there, sphinxlike, just staring at her. "So," she says in mock defiance, "what are you lookin' at?"

Chris does not even blink. "I'm lookin' at—*you!*" he replies.

Then, as Dana's eyes widen in shock, he bounds out of his chair and over the coffee table to get to her. Dana screams with laughter. She has barely had time to uncross her legs before he grabs her by the shoulders, lifts her up, and kisses her passionately. While he reaches around to unhook her bra, she undoes his belt . . .

Frozen. Chris awakened this morning in Bedford at the usual time—around six-thirty—feeling frozen, or as he put it, "more like stone than flesh." Notwithstanding the whoosh of his ventilator, Chris could hear Dana breathing softly as she slept in the bed next to his. She would sleep for another hour—time during which Chris tried to come to terms with the reality of what he called his "situation."

"I'm never disabled in my dreams," he said. "I'm never in a wheelchair. *Never.* I'm always whole—sailing, riding, traveling, making films. So naturally, I'm happiest when I'm asleep. I'm saddest each morning when I wake up."

Eventually, Chris would discover a way to push the darkest thoughts out of his mind by staring up through the skylight at the tops of the trees and concentrating on the day ahead. But for now, this hour when he was alone with his thoughts was sheer torture, devoted almost entirely to replaying the senseless accident that had robbed him and his family of so many things. "What people don't know about is, like, in the morning," he said, "when I need . . . I need twenty minutes to cry."

"Chris is incredibly resilient," Dana said at the time. "He will occasionally get down, hit rock bottom. I just listen and try to find things that can help. Close physical contact is helpful."

Indeed, one of the things that had changed drastically was the Reeves' sex life. Yet even before Chris left Kessler, he and Dana had explored the ways they could still be intimate. Once it was determined that, despite his near-complete paralysis, the accident had not rendered Chris impotent, Chris and Dana were not shy about sharing the news.

"My wife gets a lot of attention," Chris told Larry King. "She walks through the room and I'm practically leering at her." As for the all-too-obvious physical reaction: "It's really embarrassing. It's an automatic reflex. So it works. You know that thing about how it has a mind of its own? That's true!"

Chris told Katie Couric that he was "feeling like a high school senior these days."

"Oh, really?" Couric shot back. "Feeling a little randy, are we?"

While Chris's spinal injury meant that he was incapable of actually feeling anything, these "reflex erections" meant that he could have sexual relations leading to orgasm. More important, it meant that he could father more children—something both Reeves were now seriously considering.

"So, it would be possible?" Barbara Walters asked Dana.

"Yes. In fact," Dana replied, "it is possible."

"In fact, it is possible?" Walters said, somewhat taken aback by the Reeves' candor on this delicate subject.

"Yes, I'm here to tell you," Dana stated firmly, "we can, and we are able to." For the next few years, they would kick around the idea of adding to the family. But Chris and Dana were also wary of doing anything to rob Will, Matthew, and Alexandra of the attention they deserved. Moreover, Dana wondered if she could handle the added responsibility. "Quite honestly," she said, "there have been a couple of times I've been maxed out and thought, *Could I really add a screaming baby to this equation? I'd lose it!*"

It was a simple fact of their new lives that would be the de-
ciding factor. It was bad enough that Chris could no longer so
much as give Will a hug; he at least had memories of doing so.
"The idea of bringing a child into the world that he couldn't
hold or even touch," Dana said, "was just too painful for Chris."

No longer able to have sex in what he called "the ordinary way,"
Chris conceded that he missed the physical relationship he'd had
with Dana "terribly. But there are marriages where the couple are
making love all the time, but they're not really as intimate as they
should be. You know, it's a ritual, somehow not that fulfilling. But,
oddly enough, Dana and I are just as intimate as we ever were, and
that's what really counts."

It fell to Dana to create those intimate, even erotic moments.
While they slept in their spacious master bedroom, a nurse in another part of the house monitored Chris's breathing. This loss of
privacy—the fact that they were never really alone, not even as
they slept—wore heavily on Dana. "Having people in our bedroom in the morning and at night," she said, "that's the stuff that
gets to me sometimes . . ." Several times a week, they turned off
the monitors so they could have some degree of privacy, and
Dana would climb into bed beside Chris and carefully place his
arm around her.

They continued to make love, although Dana admitted "it's
nothing like our sex life was before." Since Chris was paralyzed
from the shoulders down, she said, "sex is kind of one-sided.
What we do is physically intimate, but it is not as fulfilling in
many ways for either of us. That's one of the things we miss most
of all."

Yet Dana would frequently concede that, even more than sex, what she missed most was Chris's touch. "Not being able to touch is very hard on Chris and me," Dana once conceded, fighting back tears. "It's hard to see other people do what we used to do. Even hold hands. Even, you know, I look at other couples laughing . . . a husband sort of flipping his wife's hair."

As for their sexual relationship: "It's not what it used to be," she conceded, "but it's still nice, just being close in the same bed. It's the hardest time, though, because it reminds me of what we had. I can be so strong and have this willpower all day where I say, 'It's fine, I'm fine.' And I block out the need. But when you do open yourself up to wanting that affection, you're so vulnerable. It's so lovely—you forget how lovely it can be. And then it's so painful, so bittersweet."

Chris was not unaware of Dana's pain. She was, after all, still a young woman—just thirty-four at the time of Chris's accident. "You didn't sign on for this," he often told her.

Unbowed, Dana worked hard at creating those intimate husband-and-wife moments throughout the day. "You've got to remember that it was all up to her," one of their longtime nurses said. "She was always touching him, stroking him, kissing him, leaning on his shoulder. And the wonder of it was that it was always genuine affection—it never seemed phony or forced."

Among other things, Dana often shampooed Chris's hair because, she explained, "it's a sexy, intimate thing." Chris agreed. As he was leaned back over the sink, Dana would sing to Chris as she poured shampoo over his hair and then slowly worked the lather in with her manicured nails. Then she cupped her hand over his forehead and rinsed his hair with warm water. "Ahhh," he would sigh. "You've really earned your tip this time."

One of Dana's favorite places to be with Chris was aboard an airplane, where he could now ride sitting up in a regular seat. She would sit on the arm of the chair and put his arm around her. That way, she explained, "we would be able to talk face-to-face. I always loved that. It was like old times."

The need for close physical contact was not limited to Dana and Chris. The fact that he could not so much as touch Will was devastating for Chris. "With Will, that's where Chris and I both feel the saddest and, at the same time, most grateful," Dana explained. "Chris wants to be out playing basketball with him, giving him hugs." So Dana often put Will on Chris's lap and placed Chris's motionless arm around the boy. "It's surprisingly comforting; I know because I've done it myself."

Still, she conceded, "there's always going to be a sense of loss about what our life was. We've had to adjust all our dreams, but I have no regrets. We lead a very different life. But a good life. Everyone has a cross to bear."

April 1996 was filled with promise for both Chris and Dana. The first day of the month, Chris signed on to do the voice of King Arthur in the Warner Bros. animated feature *The Quest for Camelot.* A week later, HBO offered Chris the opportunity to direct *In the Gloaming,* a drama about a young man dying of AIDS who tries in his final days to reconcile with his parents.

None of these meant as much to Chris as the letter Dana wrote him to mark the occasion of their fourth anniversary on April 11. Her voice cracked several times as she read it aloud to him.

"My darling Toph," she began. "This path we are on is unpre-

dictable, mysterious, profoundly challenging, and, yes, even fulfilling." She went on to say she had "no regrets," that the challenges
they faced only proved to Dana how deeply she loved him, and
that she was grateful they would "follow this path together . . .
With all my heart and soul I love you."

When she finished, Dana looked up to see tears rolling down
Chris's cheeks. "I love you so much," he told her as she threw
her arms over his shoulders. "Now, can you get me a Kleenex?
God, I can't even do that . . ."

What Christopher *could* do, with Dana as his confidante and
tireless ally, was daunting. In 1996, the couple established the
Christopher Reeve Foundation to raise money for the American Paralysis Association. Reeve would prove so successful at raising both cash—more than $750,000 in the first year alone—and
public awareness that in 1999 the two organizations would
merge to become the Christopher Reeve Paralysis Foundation.

In May 1996, Chris traveled to Capitol Hill to make a direct appeal for research funds. Before lobbying Congress, however, he and
Dana dropped in on their friends in the White House, where the
Reeves convinced President Clinton to add $10 million to the Na-
tional Institute of Health's research budget.

Chris's complicated medical condition began to catch up with
him by the time he arrived on the Hill. Every three weeks his
tracheotomy tube had to be replaced so that tissue would not
grow over it—a painful procedure for Chris, since he had never
lost his ability to feel above his shoulders and upper chest. Unfortunately, he had undergone a trach replacement just prior to
leaving for Washington.

For the first few days after having a new trach put in, the

slightest jostling of the trach could cause him to lose his voice completely. His speech was fine when he met with the Clintons, but by the time he sat down in front of a panel of sympathetic senators to make the case for more research funding, Chris began to panic.

Dana placed her hand on his shoulder and told him not to worry—that if there was a problem, everyone would understand. But Chris was convinced that "all these senators were sitting there, right in my face, ready for me to say something pithy and impressive. And I felt the moment had come, and I'm bombing."

Since no one was really aware that at this point Chris was capable of speaking clearly and fluidly, his difficulty with the trach went unnoticed. Chris's appearance made headlines across the country, but he later remembered how he "went off into a corner and beat myself up about having blown my big moment."

To further the cause—and to cover health care expenses not paid for by insurance ("I work or I die")—Chris hit the lecture circuit. Over the years he would crisscross the country and even travel abroad, speaking at scores of symposiums, meetings, dinners, fund-raisers, and rallies each year. For those, he was paid between $50,000 and $60,000 each—a fee that would eventually rise to over $100,000.

If he could not be there in person, Chris would often videotape a message to be played at the event. Dana was usually on hand to offer suggestions, making sure that his hair was combed, the lighting right, and—most important—that his spirits were up. "Dana would always give him a kiss on the cheek or whisper a few words in his ear," said a crew member. "She giggled a lot, and you could tell that connection they had really kept him going."

On their home turf, Chris and Dana joined forces with Chris's doctors to battle his insurance company when they refused to pay for his nursing care. According to Chris, "they said my wife can just stay home and do it." When all else failed, he called the insurance company directly. "Listen," he told a vice president, "think about how unfair it is to expect my wife to stay home twenty-four hours a day." Finally, the insurer caved in.

Now that he was getting the round-the-clock nursing care required (one night the ventilator failed twice), Dana was free to resume her career. She had landed a small part in NBC's hugely popular *Law & Order* in 1990, and after playing a reporter in HBO's *Lifestories: Families in Crisis* series in February 1996, she returned to the *Law & Order* set in the role of an ill-fated wife later that year.

Dana would go on to appear in other episodes of *Law & Order,* and when *L&O* executive producer Dick Wolf created a new series for CBS called *Feds,* he offered Dana a plum role—Meg Shelby, the sexy Republican bond trader who falls in love with the show's FBI agent protagonist. "Meg seems to be everything he's looking for in a woman," Dana said of her character, "but there's a real coldness to her that is not initially obvious." As for so obviously being cast against type, Dana cracked to her fellow actors, "I *love* it. There are times when you just wanna be a little bad, you know?"

As she eased back into the working world, Dana realized she would have to make some adjustments in terms of the kinds of projects she pursued. Before Chris's accident, for example, she had appeared in several TV commercials, including a long-running spot for Tide detergent. But now that she was the well-known spouse of a high-profile public advocate, she did not want to appear to be actually endorsing a product using the Reeve name. By way of a compromise, she began doing voice-overs.

Owning up to a little blatant nepotism, Chris also hired Dana to sing the haunting theme for *In the Gloaming*. He hired four-year-old Will, as well, to play the main character as a small child in one brief scene. These were two of the few easy choices he would be faced with during the making of the HBO film. Risking the possibility that HBO might withdraw the offer altogether, Chris agreed to direct the movie only if the script was completely rewritten. This was followed by the inevitable casting wars; Chris wanted and ultimately got Glenn Close, Robert Sean Leonard, David Strathairn, Bridget Fonda, and Whoopi Goldberg.

On the set, Chris stationed himself in front of a video monitor and, using a microphone and headset, directed each scene from there. He was so riveted by his actors that when Dana leaned over and kissed him, he only paused long enough to say, "Oh, hi!"

Dana, despite the demands of being a mother and a working actress, was a near-constant presence during the making of *In the Gloaming*. "Just to see him working again," she told one of the cast members, "is so wonderful. All the headaches and arguments and technical problems—he's in heaven!" When it aired in early 1997, Chris was stunned by the overwhelming praise from the critics. Dana, not so much. "They think you're a great director?" she joked. "Tell me something I didn't know."

In the Gloaming went on to be nominated for five Emmys and won four Cable Ace awards. Yet Chris was most touched by the congratulatory calls and visits from such fellow filmmakers as

Steven Spielberg, Herb Ross, Martin Scorsese, Peter Bogdanovich, and Francis Ford Coppola. "They were welcoming me into the fraternity of directors," he said. "I'm starting a new chapter in my life, and you have no idea how much that means."

Even as they made their joint transition back to their chosen profession, Chris and Dana continued their husband-and-wife crusade on behalf of the disabled. In July, to prove to himself as well as the rest of the world that even a quadriplegic could find a way to participate in sports, Chris returned to the high seas.

Before he agreed to compete in the Wall Street Challenge Cup regatta for the disabled off Newport, Rhode Island, Chris was warned that the risks were substantial. Any sort of bump could result in spasming or worse, even a bruise could lead to a life-threatening infection, and of course there was always the issue of a malfunctioning ventilator.

Dana had lived through all of Chris's medical emergencies, and worried aloud about the possible dangers of sailing in his condition. But once she was assured that every precaution would be taken, Dana urged Chris to "go for it." She later explained that she felt sailing aboard their yacht the *Sea Angel* "was something that we both loved and that he missed terribly. Just seeing his eyes light up when he talks about getting back out on the water . . ."

As he waited on the dock to be lifted onboard the America's Cup sloop *Northern Lights,* Chris could scarcely contain himself. "I am like an excited schoolboy," he said. "I can't wait to get on the waves again!"

The logistics were, as always, daunting. Despite the fact that Hurricane Bertha was churning up seas at it bore down on the coast, Chris and his wheelchair were hoisted aboard the *Northern Lights* using a specially designed boom as Dana watched nervously. The process took forty minutes, and once Chris was on deck, Dana rushed up to give him a hug. Then Chris's wheelchair was tightly secured to the deck next to the boat's captain.

Two of the three events planned for the day were canceled as the waves reached twelve feet, but Chris was able to compete in one ninety-minute race. With a sweater-clad Dana perched at his side, shivering in the cold as he gave orders to the *Northern Lights'* captain, Chris came in second against five other world-class sailing vessels captained by disabled sailors. The next day, he returned to the high seas, this time for a leisurely sail aboard another sloop, the *Condor,* with Dana and Will.

Dana was thrilled at what the experience had done for Chris's state of mind. "They didn't usually let people see it," said one of Chris's aides, "but there were plenty of times where he got very down, very depressed and moody. Dana worried a lot about that."

Occasionally, Dana alluded publicly to Chris's dark moments. "There are times," she said, "when he gets so upset, blaming himself for all that has happened. I tell him that of course it was just an accident that could have happened to anybody, but in the end he's the one who has to deal with those feelings."

At the same time, Dana was quick to point out that Chris never succumbed to despair. "Chris has courage people don't even know about," she said to writer Ileane Rudolph. "Daily physical and emotional struggles abound. His bravery affects me in a profound way. He is still a passionate partner and a loving, involved father, even under the worst circumstances."

For her part, Dana never lost her own wry sense of humor. At a movie premiere, her old friend, the playwright Donald Margulies, spotted an elegantly dressed Dana standing next to Chris's wheelchair. She was feeding him crudité from a plate.

"Dana, how *are* you?" Margulies asked.

"OK," Dana replied with a shrug, "*considering* . . ."

Chris, who met with scientists to keep abreast of the latest advances in spinal cord research, was especially hopeful that summer of 1996. "Awareness of spinal-cord injury is at an all-time high," he said in a *TIME* magazine cover story headlined, simply, "SUPER MAN." "People now understand that something that was thought incurable can be cured. The politicians are motivated, the scientists are motivated," he told writer Roger Rosenblatt. "Now the question is how to keep the momentum going."

Chris hosted the "Paralympics" for disabled athletes in Atlanta that August, and then went on the *Today* show to proclaim that he not only expected to walk by the time he was fifty, but that by then he fully intended to be playing tennis—and winning. Later that same day, with Dana looking proudly on from the presidential box next to then–First Lady Hillary Clinton, Chris gave the opening night speech at the 1996 Democratic National Convention in Chicago. Again, the audience of several thousand was moved to tears as the actor who once soared as Superman made an emotional plea for the government to do more for the disabled.

Urging his country to "take care of our family and not slash programs people need," Chris invoked the name of another famous wheelchair-bound American to drive home his point. "President Roosevelt shows us that a man who could barely lift himself out of a wheelchair could still lift a nation out of despair." During Chris's emotional twenty-minute-long speech, the crowd leaped to its feet cheering more than a dozen times.

Two days after the convention ended, the Reeves were back home when they learned along with the rest of the world that Princess Diana had been killed in a Paris car crash. Chris and the princess had danced at the party following the London premiere of *Superman II* nearly two decades earlier, and he treasured her letters of support. "I'll always remember dancing with you," Diana wrote Chris just weeks after his accident, "and I hope someday we'll dance together again. If anyone can do it, you can."

Chris and Dana both kept up with the latest research by inviting the leading experts to visit them at their home in Bedford. "Most important, Chris has brought a new enthusiasm to the scientists," American Paralysis Association president Mitchell Stoler said. "He's inspired them."

For his part, Chris did not shrink from his new role as a champion of the disabled. Not that it was a task he would have sought out. "It seems," he told Dana, "I've become president of a club I never wanted to join."

It was in that capacity that Chris narrated the Emmy-winning *Without Pity: A Film About Abilities,* part of HBO's *America Undercover* series. He declined to appear on camera, fearing that his presence might distract from the stories of the disabled people profiled in the documentary.

Chris felt almost as shy about showing up for the first Christopher Reeve Foundation fund-raising gala in his hometown of

Princeton. On January 12, 1997, some twelve hundred people showed up at Princeton's McCarter Theatre—the very theater where Chris first appeared in Gilbert and Sullivan's *The Yeoman of the Guard* at the age of nine—to honor Chris. Among the performers: Carly Simon, Mandy Patinkin, John Lithgow, and Chris's Princeton Day schoolmate Mary Chapin Carpenter.

"I think God sent Chris to be the man to do this," Patinkin said of his old Juilliard classmate, "because of his heart and courage and awareness and fight. The ironies are unbelievable. He's more than Superman."

Perhaps. But Chris felt somewhat uneasy about appearing before his childhood friends and neighbors. "While I have very wonderful memories of growing up in Princeton, I've not been good at staying in touch . . ." Besides, he added, "people have gone to so much trouble for me. I'm grateful for it, but I get a little embarrassed."

Still, he admitted that Princeton "absolutely formed me. It set me on a path that brought me great, great happiness." When all the stars gathered onstage and Dana took the microphone to lead the audience in singing "Getting to Know You" from Rodgers and Hammerstein's *The King and I,* Chris was "floored. I guess the prerequisite to living in Princeton," he said of the crowd's spirited performance, "is that you have to be able to sing."

At the party afterward, Dana, wearing a simple gold wedding ring and diamond solitaire earrings (a Christmas present from Chris), placed a shawl around her shoulders and went in search of fruit juice for her husband. She returned moments later and bent over Chris, gently placing the straw in his mouth. After a few sips, he nodded that he had had enough. With that, she knelt down and placed her face against his. They both closed their eyes for a moment. "Mmmmm," he said, smiling sweetly, "warm cheek."

Three days after his emotional Princeton homecoming, Chris was sitting in his family room watching Will and Dana play floor hockey with plastic golf clubs and a large bottle cap for a puck. As usual, at various points in the game the players stepped aside as Chris and his wheelchair became the Zamboni, carefully resurfacing the "ice." It was then that Chris noticed that his left leg was beginning to swell. Dana rushed him to the emergency room at Northern Westchester Hospital, where doctors raced against time to save him from a life-threatening blood clot behind his left knee. Chris was promptly put on blood thinners designed to break up up the clot, which could have proved fatal if it had traveled to his lungs.

Throughout the ordeal, said one of the nurses, Dana was "clutching Chris's hand and praying. We were all praying." After a week, he was released from the hospital—only to be readmitted when the clot reappeared.

Not long after he returned home from his second hospital stay, Chris was being lifted from his exercise bicycle back into his wheelchair by two aides when suddenly he crashed to the floor. Dana, who had been talking with Chris while he sat on the exercycle, rushed to help put him back in his wheelchair. When she did, she noticed that his left arm was now dangling oddly. "That doesn't look good, hon," she said with a sympathetic wince.

X-rays soon revealed that Chris's upper arm had suffered a clean break in the fall—so clean ("like a matchstick," Chris said) that surgeons would have to insert a titanium rod inside the bone to join the two pieces. During the successful operation, Chris would nevertheless wind up losing a considerable amount of blood—in this case four pints, or about 25 percent of the body's normal supply. Nevertheless, two days later he showed up at a special screening of *In the Gloaming* at New York's Museum of Modern Art.

No sooner had he recovered from this latest setback than Chris received word that he would be receiving a star on the Hollywood Walk of Fame—the result of pressure from INSITE, the 10,000-member-strong International Network of *Somewhere in Time* Enthusiasts. On April 15, 1997, Reeve's *Somewhere in Time* costar Jane Seymour joined Glenn Close in paying tribute to Chris at the dedication. While Dana stood next to her husband in the broiling California sun, Will rested his head in Chris's lap. Whenever the crowd applauded, Will slapped his hand against his dad's.

By this time, Chris had begun to regain some faint sense of feeling in his arms, hands, and back. That meant Chris could "feel Will's hand on mine. I feel his arm on mine . . . The thing I want more, though, is to be able to put my arms around him. That's what he's entitled to. That's what Dana is entitled to."

That spring, Dana watched proudly from the sidelines as more honors were heaped on her husband. On May 18, Chris delivered an emotional commencement address to the Boston University School of Medicine's graduating class. Paraphrasing the famous line from *Jerry Maguire,* Reeve, who was awarded an honorary doctorate by the prestigious institution, demanded, "Show us the cures!"

At a fund-raiser in Puerto Rico that same month, Chris

showed a film clip of laboratory rats that had had their spinal cords completely severed and were then given an experimental drug. Incredibly, within a month the nerves had regenerated to such an extent that the rats were scampering about. "Oh, to be a rat," Chris told the audience.

"They laughed," Dana said, "but he meant it." When asked if he was willing to participate in the first human trials for such drugs, he answered unhesitatingly, "Of course. Are you kidding?!"

In the meantime, Dana marveled at her husband's stamina. "He is the most energetic and involved person I've ever known," she observed. "He wakes up every morning ready to tackle the world."

Not that he didn't have moments when he just wanted to shut the door and tell everyone to go away. "I liked it better," he often said, "when my life was shallow."

Chris's characteristic exuberance and unbridled enthusiasm belied the perilous state of his health—and Dana's keen awareness that at any moment disaster might strike. On Memorial Day weekend, exactly two years after Chris's near-fatal accident, the Reeves decamped to Williamstown. A few days later, Dana noticed that one of Chris's shoes had caused a small irritation on his left ankle. Within a month, the irritation had become so badly infected that it traveled to the bone; doctors feared that, in order to save his life, they would have to amputate Chris's foot. After surgery to remove the infected tissue, Chris was given massive doses of antibiotics, to which he promptly developed an allergic reaction. It would be seven months after Dana first spotted the small red irritation on Chris's ankle before doctors could finally stop treating it.

On June 30, the Reeves paused to mark a special anniversary. "It's hard to believe we've been together as a couple for ten years,"

Dana said, "because we're still so in love. It's nice to honestly feel I have no regrets. A terrible thing happened. I wish it hadn't. But would I change who I married? Never."

Still, as they ricocheted from one crisis to another, Dana never let on to Chris just how worried she was. "My problems are very different from his," she once explained. "Mine are the problems of someone who is married to a man who is paralyzed. But he is the one who has to sit in that chair." She was not, she continued, "going to add to his troubles by looking upset."

Toward that end, she had also given up horseback riding in the wake of Chris's accident. "I rode my whole life," she said, "but he loved it so much, it really would have been painful for him if I was going off riding and he wasn't able to."

What he was able to do physically—what Chris and Dana both believed he needed to do—was to go through his punishing exercise regimen to maintain muscle tone. "If a breakthrough in spinal regeneration comes," he said succinctly, "it won't do me any good if my muscles have atrophied."

"Atrophy" was the last word anyone would have applied to either Chris or Dana during this challenging period in their lives. In early 1998, they both appeared with such celebrity friends as Tom Hanks, Paul McCartney, Meryl Streep, Willie Nelson, and Stevie Wonder in *Christopher Reeve: A Celebration of Hope,* an ABC-TV prime-time variety special benefiting the Christopher Reeve Foundation.

Chris was suffering from laryngitis and an upper respiratory infection, but he smiled gamely as each star took to the stage. None would have more of an impact on the audience—or on Chris— than Dana. After she sang "The Music That Makes Me Dance," she explained its significance. "It's special for us," she said wistfully as Chris looked on. "It's the song I sang the night Chris and I met."

Soon after, Chris and Dana hit the road together to promote *Still Me,* the memoir he had started working on three years earlier at the Kessler Institute. Each day at the Reeves' gray-shingled house in Bedford, he would dictate his thoughts to an assistant as he stared out the window at the small pond they shared with their neighbor. "I had no notes," he said, "but the odd thing is how sharp my memory has become. Since I can't move and have so many fewer distractions, my memory is keener . . . It's easier to focus my thoughts because I haven't other things to do." The book wound up spending eleven weeks on the *New York Times* Best Seller List, while the audio version earned Chris a Grammy for Best Spoken Word Album.

It marked the last time Dana would ever talk in detail about Chris's accident. "It's such a stark before-and-after—the point at which our lives really changed," she mused. "It's so painful—really, really painful—that I only talked about it that one time. I won't ever do it again."

It was while promoting the book that Chris and Dana—who inscribed thousands of copies of *Still Me* on her husband's behalf with the words "Christopher Reeve by Dana Reeve"—reluctantly came to the conclusion once and for all that they would not try to have more children. "If things were different," Dana said, "we probably would have another child, but they are not. I really want to make sure that the kids who are around are OK."

For Chris, the reason for not having a child was simple. "I'm not sure I could handle having a little baby," he told Dana, "that I will never be able to pick up and hold." After all, it had been three years since Chris had been able to put his arms around Will. "And there are times when he *needs* a hug from me. But the best he can do is come over and lean on my shoulder."

In truth, Dana would harbor some concerns about Will after he enrolled in the first grade. "There are times when he has real separation anxiety, and wants me around," she acknowledged. She enlisted the help of Matthew, now a sophomore at Brown University in Rhode Island, and Alexandra, who would soon be attending Yale, in shoring up Will's self-confidence. Soon Will would be using the nickname both Matthew and Alex had bestowed on Dad. To them, he was "The Big Cheese."

In the wake of what had happened to Will's father, Dana and Chris were determined to resist the urge to be overprotective. Understandably concerned about any activities that might result in a spinal cord injury, they warned Will about diving into shallow water and prohibited him from playing on trampolines. Beyond that, however, they encouraged Will to play team sports like hockey. "The more skilled you become at something, the safer you are," Dana reasoned. There was an added benefit: watching baseball, basketball, and hockey on television became a favorite father-son pastime.

Unable to do many of the standard things a dad does with his son—play catch, kick around a soccer ball, or simply roughhouse—Chris seized every opportunity he could to be part of Will's life. He parked his wheelchair near the pool to give Will swimming tips ("Now lift your arms up out of the water more . . . Now don't forget to keep kicking.") and in the driveway to teach him how to ride a bike ("Keep your feet on the pedals . . . Look out for that tree!").

"I want to set him free," Chris said of Will. "I want him to be a kid so when he goes out of the house every morning he's not worried about the old man."

In lieu of expanding their family, both Dana and Chris flexed their creative muscles. In the fall of 1998, he tackled his first acting role since the accident—as the wheelchair-bound peeping Tom in ABC's prime-time remake of the Alfred Hitchcock classic *Rear Window*. Unlike the James Stewart character in the original, a man recovering from a broken leg who happens to witness a murder while peering into neighboring apartments with binoculars, Chris wanted to be a "vent-dependent quadriplegic living in an apartment with the latest assistive techniques." His character, a former architect "with an outsize ego," would come to see the accident that paralyzed him as "a lesson in humility. He starts out as a master of the universe," Chris said as someone speaking from experience, "and he goes through a profound transformation."

Chris, who would also coproduce the movie, rejected the first script as "too melodramatic and medically inaccurate." Instead, he incorporated harrowing elements from his own life—like a scene in which the hero suffers a ventilator pop-off and has to summon help by clicking his tongue.

Still, he "worried that only acting with my voice and my face, I might not be able to communicate effectively enough to tell the story. But," he said, "I was surprised to find that if I really concentrated, and just let the thoughts happen, that they would read on my face." His peers apparently agreed; Chris edged out fellow nominees James Garner, Charles S. Dutton, Ben Kingsley, Ray Liotta, and Stanley Tucci to win a Screen Actors Guild Award as Best Actor in a Miniseries or Television Movie.

While Chris worked on *Rear Window*, Dana realized a lifelong dream. In October 1998, she made her Broadway debut, as a Long Island housewife married to a comedian in Rob Bartlett's play *More to Love: A Big Fat Comedy*.

"She was an incredibly gifted comedienne," said Bartlett, who played her husband in *More to Love*. "She auditioned for the show by singing 'Do You Know the Way to San Jose?' while she did this little drama like she was driving a car. It was sweet and quirky and funny, and we knew right away she was the one. There was something almost Lucy-esque about her. I remember wondering why no one had put her on Broadway before."

The show's director, Jack O'Brien, agreed. "Dana had what G. B. Shaw called that 'spark of divine fire.' She was definitely a player. But if she gave up a lot of opportunities to care for Chris, she was never anxious or self-pitying. She did what she did because she *wanted* to. She was deeply in love with Chris."

The reality of actually making it to Broadway finally hit Dana when she watched as her name was spelled out on the marquee of the Eugene O'Neill Theater. "It's thrilling to walk in the stage door," she conceded, "because then you know you belong."

Chris was on hand opening night, dressed in a dark gray suit. He had urged Dana to take the role and even helped her rehearse her lines—proud, he said, "because it's time she got the attention she deserves . . . I've overshadowed her a little." But after just four performances, *More to Love* closed. After the final performance, Dana and some of the actors from the show went to Joe Allen's, the legendary Broadway hangout that boasts a "Wall of Shame" covered with the posters of shows that ran ten performances or less. On the way, Dana ripped a *More to Love* poster off the side of a flower stand so they could take it to the restaurant and autograph it personally before it went up on the Wall of Shame. "She said she was proud of the show and all our work," Bartlett recalled. "As if you hadn't fallen in love with her already . . ."

Like virtually everyone who encountered her, Bartlett, who worked up to eighteen hours a day with Dana for months, said Dana was "an inspiration. She changed me, just by the example she set." He recalled that a favorite line of Dana's was "Don't expect life to be easy," and, Bartlett noted, "she knew that better than anyone. But she kept going. I never knew anyone with a stronger sense of who she was."

As she had so many times before, Dana handled this latest setback with grace and humor. "Gee," she told Chris when she got home to Bedford, "I was in a longer-running show when I was a snowflake in the third-grade Christmas pageant."

No matter. Two weeks after *More to Love* folded, Chris was again sitting proudly in the audience as Dana accepted Procter & Gamble's Shining Example Award for her "grace, courage, and activism"—along with a $25,000 check for the Christopher Reeve Foundation.

That Thanksgiving 1998, the Reeves had more to be grateful for than awards and juicy parts in plays and movies. In September, Chris had easily blown out the single candle on his birthday cake—something he had been unable to do for the first three years following his accident.

There was more: At one point that year, Dana heard a strange, explosive sound coming from Chris's office and ran in to check it out. "What was that?" she asked.

"I sneezed!" he replied happily. "I really sneezed!" Dana and the nurses cheered, and with good reason: Sneezing is a sudden, violent contraction of the diaphragm, which atrophies with paralysis and disuse. Although his pre-accident sneeze "would knock down walls," Chris not been able to sneeze since the accident. The fact that he could now sneeze was a definite sign that the breathing exercises he had been doing to wean himself of the ventilator were working.

By this time, Chris was able to fully appreciate the way in which his redefined life had brought his entire family closer. Nearly all the time he had spent before with his brothers and sisters, for example, had been devoted to skiing, sailing, playing tennis, or tossing around a football. "Now," he reflected, "because physical activities are limited, we spend hours talking to each other instead of being busy doing things." Not that he ever felt excluded when the family did decide to get physical: During the Reeves' annual Thanksgiving Day soccer game, it was Chris who made the calls as referee.

In 1999, Dana followed Chris onto the Best Seller List with *Care Packages: Letters to Christopher Reeve from Strangers and Other Friends.* Dedicated to "Will, my most precious care package," Dana's first book was a sampling of the letters Chris had received since his accident—thoughts and prayers from stars like Hepburn, Robert De Niro, John Travolta, Hugh Grant, Arnold Schwarzenegger, Emma Thompson, and Paul McCartney, to Bill and Hillary Clinton, Nancy Reagan, and even the men on San Quentin's Death Row ("We're not all tough guys. We love you, Chris."). The most touching were from young Superman fans: "I'm sorry that you fell off your horse. Let's hope it won't happen again."

For Dana, *Care Packages* was "a thank-you letter. A long over-due reply to all of the people who . . . prayed for us, joined hands for us . . . cried for us, cheered for us, sent positive energy our way." The book was also, said Dana, a love letter—"a love letter to Chris from me." (She would write the foreword for another epistolary collection, *Love Letters of a Lifetime,* two years later.)

That success was offset by yet another medical setback when, the same week *Care Packages* was released in October 1999, a der-matologist noticed a lesion on Chris's arm. It turned out to be skin cancer. Fortunately, it was caught early enough for Chris to be treated and cured. "Dana was very, very concerned, of course," said one of Chris's nurses. "But she never let on for a minute."

Dana was, in fact, becoming increasingly celebrated as a kind of hero, if not a saint. She was now routinely being called "Saint Dana," "Superwoman," or America's "Caretaker-in-Chief." Each sobriquet made her wince. "I am not a hero," she said with a laugh, "and I am most certainly not a saint! There's nothing su-perhuman about standing by Chris. What's so saintly about that? Lucky me. I'm with him!"

Surprisingly, sometimes the smallest things were the biggest re-minders of what she'd lost: There was no one to help latch her bracelet, no one to warm up the car, no one to hand the baby to. "All these little things that people don't think about," she said. "You are really on your own and, not only that, you're caring for someone. It's years and years. Your entire life has really changed. Are you up for the task?"

At Dana's insistence, she and Chris each began seeing a ther-apist. "There are some things that I don't think you should share with your spouse," she explained. "You get a heart doctor for your heart. A therapist is an emotion doctor for your emotions."

Like her husband, Dana considered herself "very fortunate because I have a tremendous amount of help and love and support from people I don't even know. There are millions of people who are caring for loved ones under much, much worse circumstances and they go completely unheralded. I thought, *Really, my job here is to be the voice for the many, many spouses who are caregivers, who don't have the advantage of the world patting them on the back every day.* I'm not a saint. I'm a voice for the silent partner."

There was another, unforeseen consequence to being lauded as a nurturer: "The one downside," she said, "is that people perceive me as way older than I am. I used to audition for sexier roles, and then suddenly I'm only called to play the beleaguered wife." In desperation, she called her agent. "Please tell people," Dana said, "that I'm younger than Meg Ryan!"

In 2000, Dana turned down a part in the Broadway musical *The Full Monty* because it would have required leaving home for the six-month tryout in San Diego. "He's an incredible human being," she said of her decision to stay by Chris's side. "Who wouldn't want to be with him?"

She did take acting jobs in the New York area, however. In addition to another appearance on *Law & Order,* Dana landed a recurring role as a politician's campaign manager in the gritty HBO prison drama *Oz.* She also joined veteran ABC newswoman Deborah Roberts as cohost of a Lifetime network talk show, *Lifetime Live.* Dana agreed to do the show because it aired live at noon, which meant that she could drive to the Astoria Studios in Queens, do the show, leave at 2 P.M., and be back before Will returned from school at four. "I can still be a stay-at-home wife and mom," she said beaming, "and have a *real* job!"

This "real job" could sometimes get to her. "We all knew she had those extra challenges in her life," said Deborah Roberts. "She handled them happily, with aplomb." Dana cracked only once, just as she was about to interview a woman who had lost a child. In the walk-up to the interview, producers showed a video of the woman at the funeral; her surviving child was comforting her by stroking her face. "Dana just lost it," recalled Roberts. "She couldn't stop crying." The video reminded Dana of how Will had tried to comfort her in the aftermath of Chris's accident.

Dana's hopes for Chris's recovery were now rather modest. "I'd love it," she said, "if he could gain some more arm motion back so he could drive, or if he could get off his ventilator. Then we could go out to dinner without another person."

"Every step of their journey, Dana saw around the corner first," Peter Kiernan said. "She accepted the reality of the situation. You know the stages of death—anger, denial, bargaining, acceptance? Well, Chris never got past bargaining to acceptance. He was going to fight until the end."

The strength of their relationship, they both insisted, was not dependent on Chris's recovery. "Dana never makes me feel guilty about creating this situation," he said. "We're just as much in love. Whether I have zero recovery or full recovery, our relationship will survive. That's pretty incredible."

That said, Chris seemed more confident than ever that he would regain the use of his legs. That dream was brought home dramatically in January 2000, when an estimated 150 million viewers tuned into the Super Bowl and saw a handsome, tuxedo-clad Christopher Reeve appear to rise from his chair and walk in a commercial for Nuveen Investments. Chris loved the spot, which, thanks to a little technical magic, was so convincing that it sent thousands of paralysis victims and their family members to their phones. They wanted to know how they could cure their spinal cord injury the way Reeve had cured his.

While the ad was widely criticized as misleading, Chris and Dana both stood by it. "This," he said, "is a motivating vision of something that can actually happen." Nor was Chris, who still shouldered crushing medical bills, about to turn his nose up at the $1 million Nuveen had paid him for the ad.

These days, the financial pressures were such that Chris was accepting offers from Madison Avenue. He was paid another $1 million to endorse an on-line supplemental health insurance firm, HealthExtras. He also directed corporate image ads for Johnson & Johnson, including one heart-tugging spot about faith that he also appeared in. "Tell your kids," he said, "that with faith, bad days will become good days in disguise."

Faith was something Chris and Dana knew quite a lot about. Yet neither was religious in the conventional sense. Dana, who had been raised a practicing Catholic, drifted away from the church in her twenties. As a child in Princeton, Chris attended Presbyterian services most Sundays, but wound up experimenting with Scientology in 1975 before embarking on his own lengthy spiritual quest.

Chris's first true act of faith, he was proud of saying, was not a religious one. It occurred the day he threw off his lifelong fear of commitment and married Dana. Three years later, after waking up paralyzed in a Virginia hospital, Chris once again found himself grappling not only with his own mortality but with spiritual issues. When he told his friend Bobby Kennedy, Jr., that he felt "like a phony" praying to a God he had never acknowledged in the past, Kennedy told him to "fake it till you make it . . . Your faith will become real soon enough."

Chris and Dana did find a religion that reflected their humanist values—Unitarian Universalism—and by the turn of the new millennium were attending services regularly. Dana shared Chris's abiding belief that "God is love," and they both were fond of citing Abraham Lincoln's answer when he was asked about his religious affiliation. "When I do good I feel good. When I do bad I feel bad. That," said Lincoln, "is my religion."

Hollywood was so impressed with the good Chris and Dana had done that half of it turned out to honor them at the annual Christopher Reeve Foundation benefit held on August 16, 2000 in Beverly Hills. Ben Affleck, Samuel L. Jackson, George Clooney, Michael Douglas, Catherine Zeta-Jones, Goldie Hawn, Michael J. Fox, and then–First Daughter Chelsea Clinton were among those who showed up to help raise more than $2 million.

The next morning, Dana and Chris arrived at the UCLA Medical Center, where he started several days of aggressive physical therapy. Held up by a harness and with electrodes stimulating involuntary contractions in his legs, Chris was able to "walk" on a treadmill. The operating theory: that "activity-dependent training," as it was called, could awaken dormant pathways in the spinal cord.

Four days later, while he was being lifted from his wheelchair, Chris fell yet again. This time, he slammed his body against a table. Because he was now suffering from severe osteoporosis, the impact was enough to shatter his left thigh. Using the alias Christopher Johnson, Chris checked into Suite No. 8 in the west wing of UCLA Medical Center's Intensive Care Unit. His nurse and personal assistant were on hand, but it fell to Dana, as it always did, to bolster his flagging spirits. "She was telling him everything was going to be OK, that he was going to be back on the treadmill in no time," said one of the UCLA nurses. "But then they'd let their guard down for a minute, and seeing the disappointment in their eyes just made you want to cry."

Five days after the doctors had fastened Chris's left femur using pins and a metal rod, the Reeves flew back home to Bedford. Undaunted, Chris resumed his grueling physical therapy regimen. With Dana cheering him on, he improved rapidly. By October, he was fit enough to hit the presidential campaign trail on behalf of his old friend and fellow environmental activist Al Gore.

Then, as Dana sat chatting with Chris late one afternoon in November 2000, she noticed something odd: As he was emphatically making a point, the index finger on Chris's left hand was moving.

"Are you doing that on purpose?" she asked.

"No," he replied.

"Well," she said, reaching down to pet their yellow Labrador retriever Chamois, "*try.*"

If it had been anyone other than Dana, Chris would not have tried. It had been five years since he was able to move anything below his shoulders, and as he often admitted, "I don't like to fail."

Instead, he looked down at the finger and concentrated on establishing a connection with it. He focused on the finger for a long time, and Dana waited patiently. But when it looked to him as if she was about to "get up and go into the other room to make dinner," Chris commanded his finger to move. It did, tapping on the armrest until he shouted "Stop!" And it did.

Dana jumped up and ran over to Chris, staring down at his hand. Chris did it again. A third time, Dana gave the order to move—and again it did. Then Chris did it with his eyes closed.

Dana grabbed Chris and held him tight, her eyes filling with tears.

"Where is this coming from?" Dana asked, incredulous. "How is it possible?"

They called for Chris's head nurse, Dolly Arro, who started shouting when she saw Chris move his finger. "No way! No way!" she yelled, and got on the phone to one of his physicians, Dr. Harlan Weinberg.

Chris turned to Dana. "At least," he said, "it's good for a party trick."

Not long after, Chris was in New Orleans to give the keynote speech at the annual Symposium of Neuroscientists. While there, he spotted his old friend Dr. John McDonald, medical director of the Spinal Cord Injury Program at Washington University School of Medicine in St. Louis. When McDonald asked how he had been doing, Chris said, "I want to show you something you might find interesting." Then he matter-of-factly moved his finger.

"You would have thought," Chris recalled of McDonald's reaction, "he would not have been more astonished if I had just walked on water." Actually, McDonald soon added aquatherapy to Chris's routine. Dana and the nurses cheered as Chris, held up in the water by aides, was able to slowly kick his legs and move forward in the pool. "That was an incredible experience for me," he later said. "The fact that I actually took steps forward . . . reaffirmed my belief that I am going to walk again."

Now Chris was spending up to four hours a day on his activity-dependent workouts, spending longer periods of time on his Stim-Master and his stationary bike. He was also devoting more time to practicing his breathing off the respirator. Within a year, he would be able to move the fingers of his left hand, raise his right hand ninety degrees, breathe independently for up to ninety minutes—and wiggle all the toes on both feet. He could also feel pinpricks over 70 percent of his body, and tell the difference between hot and cold.

Most important, he could now feel it when Dana and the children hugged him. Now when Will put his hand on his father's hand, Chris could feel it just the way he used to. "To be able to feel just the slightest touch," he said, "is really a gift."

"No one who has suffered an injury as severe as Chris's," Dr. McDonald said, "and not had any initial recovery, has regained the amount of motor and sensory function he has—not even close."

Chris's progress was indeed astonishing, and he described it all in a new book, *Nothing Is Impossible,* as well as in an ABC-TV documentary, *Christopher Reeve: Courageous Steps,* directed by his son Matthew. It all made it possible for Chris to face the arrival of his fiftieth birthday on September 25, 2002—the day by which he had vowed to be walking again—with hope rather than disappointment.

To mark the date, Chris's friends threw a "Magical Birthday Bash" for Chris in New York. The celebrity-packed auction, which raised $2 million for the Christopher Reeve Foundation, was attended by several friends who shared the same birthday, including Barbara Walters, Michael Douglas, and Douglas's wife, Catherine Zeta-Jones. Yet, once again, it was Chris's old pal Robin

Williams who stole the show. "Bid five thousand dollars!" he said, pointing to Chris. "See him move his leg!" The hirsute Williams then told the black-tie crowd that he was still praying for a cure for unwanted body hair. Chris chipped in with a joke of his own: "What's the difference between Christopher Reeve and O. J. Simpson? O. J. walked."

Dana supplied the most touching moment of the evening. Utilizing Matthew's film editing skills and with Will doing the voice-over, Dana had prepared a video tribute to her husband that moved many in the audience to tears.

Throughout his private struggle to regain feeling and movement, Chris never stopped his public crusade for spinal cord research. "It's not a job I would have chosen," he said, "but one that I fully embrace because there are so many people suffering and I want to do everything I can to help." Chris continued lobbying Congress for insurance reform—he became a familiar figure, racing down the long hallways of the Capitol in his wheelchair—and pushed for pioneering rehabilitative therapies.

At the top of his agenda: stem cell research, which involved using embryonic cells to replace damaged cells. Chris's outspoken support of this research put him in direct conflict with President George W. Bush, who restricted research to those stem cell "lines" that had been created prior to August 9, 2001. In 2002, Chris, with Dana at his side, testified before the Senate on behalf of a bill allowing the research to go forward.

Dana, meantime, focused her attention on helping those who, like herself, were faced with the day-to-day burden of caregiving. "I was the one who figured out 'Is there a wheelchair ramp so that our family can get into this movie theater?' I thought if that's hard for me, it's got to be much harder for the majority of people out there."

"When people are first injured or as a disease progresses into paralysis, they don't know where to turn," Chris explained. "Dana and I wanted a facility that could give support and information to people." Added Dana, "I wanted there to be one place you could contact and ask, 'What do I do now?' and find answers."

Toward that end, they established the Christopher and Dana Reeve Paralysis Resource Center in May 2002. Dana would admit to having "a soft spot" in her heart for this and the foundation's quality-of-life grants aimed at helping paralysis victims and their families get the equipment and the services they need.

It was a theme Chris would bring to the small screen in April 2003, when he appeared on ABC's *The Practice* as a quadriplegic whose burned-out caregiver wife is accused of murder. Incredibly, only four weeks earlier Chris had undergone experimental surgery in Cleveland to have electrodes implanted in his diaphragm that would stimulate his breathing and make it possible for him to breathe off his ventilator. Chris was only the third person ever to undergo the surgery. "What do I have to lose?" he replied when asked if he was worried about the risk. "There's not much more you can do to me."

The following month, Chris was awarded the prestigious Lasker Award for Public Service "for his perceptive, sustained and heroic advocacy for medical research in general and victims of disability in particular." The jury awarding the prize went on to say that his dedication to educating himself about the scientific and political aspects of research "and his renown as an actor has allowed him to wield tremendous influence with both government officials and the public."

Chris's influence extended far beyond the borders of the U.S. Early that year, Chris and Dana had taken their first overseas trip since his accident, to Australia, where he pushed for government funding of spinal cord research Down Under. They also found time to unwind at the beach in Sydney, where Dad watched as Dana and Will frolicked in the surf.

Later, Chris would make a similar trip to Israel, where he met with Prime Minister Ariel Sharon and drew admiring crowds wherever he went—at the Yad Vashem Holocaust memorial, the Western Wall, and the hospitals where he spent time with medical researchers and the victims of terrorist attacks. Many were surprised at his appearance. The alopecia that had plagued him since his teenage years had returned with a vengeance, compounded by a reaction to medication. He disguised his patchy scalp by simply shaving his head—"My Lex Luthor look," he smiled.

Increasingly, the Reeves wanted to spend time working at the craft they loved. Chris had never stopped pushing Dana to pursue her show business career ("Go! Take the job! I'm fine. It's OK!"), and in 2003 she did four episodes of the PBS historical series *Freedom: A History of Us.* That same year, she acted in Donald Margulies's play *Two Days* at New Haven's Long Wharf Theater and off-Broadway in *Portraits,* portraying the wife of a World Trade Center office worker killed during the September 11 terrorist attacks. "She's a terrific actress and she also can bring some other elements to this role because of her own life," said the play's author, Jonathan Bell. "She identifies with this woman in a lot of ways."

Chris, meanwhile, acted in the role of Dr. Swann in the popular television series about the young Superman, *Smallville*—a role he would reprise the following year. But the project that most fascinated him was the story of a young woman named Brooke Ellison. Chris had told Dana that he wanted to direct the story of someone facing a spinal cord injury "just once," and that Ellison's was the story he wanted to tell.

Ellison became a ventilator-dependent quadriplegic when she was struck by a car in 1990 at age eleven. A decade later, she graduated summa cum laude from Harvard University with a degree in cognitive neuroscience. "I knew Chris would be able to tell my story with a sensitivity nobody else could bring," Ellison said. "To be disconnected from your ventilator and the panic that you feel, I don't think you can understand that unless you've lived it."

All the Reeves were enthusiastic about another of Chris's film projects, an animated feature called *Yankee Irving.* The Depression-era tale of an eight-year-old with a talking baseball named Screwy, *Yankee Irving* (later retitled *Everyone's Hero*) was to be directed by Chris and feature Dana in the role of Irving's mom.

Behind the scenes, the real-life drama that was the life of Chris and Dana Reeve took another turn when he was hospitalized with severe pneumonia in December 2003. Chris would recover, but only to begin battling a series of infections.

By the spring of 2004, he was no longer able to get onto his bicycle or into a pool for those exercises that had kept his muscles toned and had given him an overall sense of physical well-being. To make things worse, the huge amounts of calcium he was taking had caused massive bone growth in his hips. As a result, he could not lie on his side for more than twenty minutes at a time—all of which was making it impossible for him to sleep. "My recovery," he admitted to a British journalist, "appears to have plateaued."

Between their occasional acting and directing jobs, the speeches and the books and the medical symposia, testifying before Congress, the fund-raisers and the medical crises, Chris and Dana still made time for Will. As obsessed as Chris was with the latest advances in spinal cord research, he and Dana had one important rule when they sat down to dinner each day at 7 P.M.: "We never talk about medical issues at the table. That's strictly family time."

Dad had somehow managed to teach Will how to ride a bicycle "just by talking him through it," and coached him in baseball and hockey. He also made most of Will's games; Dana made them all. "Will had a strong relationship with Chris," Dana would later say. Because of the accident, Will grew up knowing his father as the courageous man he really was, "and didn't just see a framed photograph of Superman."

"There was definitely a celebratory quality in their raising of him," said Dana's sister Deborah. Dana and Will had "their own special thing. They were very tight. They had to stick together from a very early point. A lot of her life was being a hockey mom." So strong was their mother-son bond, that even as he approached his eleventh birthday, Dana sang Will to sleep every night.

As much as he hated to leave Will behind even for a couple of weeks, Chris still had to work. Matthew had already graduated from Brown and was pursuing his own career as a documentary filmmaker, but Alexandra was still at Yale, and for Will, college was years in the future. As for his medical expenses, the Reeves' three health insurance policies—each of which had a $1 million cap— were scheduled to run out in 2005. While he shrugged off the financial disaster that loomed on the horizon ("I'll cross that bridge when I come to it."), Chris knew he had to keep working.

That summer, Chris, accompanied by Dana, Will, and his medical support team, arrived in New Orleans to begin directing *The Brooke Ellison Story* in sweltering one-hundred-degree heat. According to Lacey Chabert, the actress who portrayed Ellison in the film, Chris "was right on top of every little detail. There were obvious physical limitations, but there were no creative limitations."

"He worked incredible hours in this unbelievable, brutal heat," recalled Ellison, who spent time on the set. "It was truly a labor of love."

One evening, Ellison and her family joined Dana, Chris, and Will for dinner at a New Orleans restaurant. "People were coming up to the table and snapping their pictures while they ate," Ellison said, "but Chris and Dana didn't seem bothered at all. They were completely gracious, relaxed and natural. The whole family was—radiant."

By the time he returned to New York, Chris had developed another infection, this time in his chest, and was by his own admission "in constant pain." It was around this time that his old friend and self-described consigliere Peter Kiernan, who also served as vice chairman of the Christopher Reeve Foundation, asked him what his plans were for the foundation in the event of his death. "You're a powerful guy," Kiernan told him. "You'll pull through like you always do, but let's talk about what happens to the foundation if you die. This organization is like the solar system with you at its center. What happens when the sun goes out?"

Chris took only a few moments to answer. "Look," he told Kiernan, "if something happens to me, Dana will definitely take on a bigger role. But I want you to help her run things."

"Chris was really a civil rights leader," Kiernan said. "The fifty million disabled people in this country cried out for what every civil rights movement cries out for—a voice. Chris was that voice. What does a movement do without its Gandhi?"

Dana waited for the infection to subside before leaving for California, where she was appearing in the Broadway-bound play *Brooklyn Boy*. She planned on returning every "actor's weekend"—Sunday through Tuesday—and was happy that Will and Chris could "really bond" in her absence—"You know, whenever I'm gone it's dad and son time."

Dana flew home for Chris's fifty-second birthday on September 25, and watched with Will, Alexandra, and Chris's mother, Barbara, as the birthday boy was presented with his "cake"—actually a bowl of the junket (milk pudding set with rennet) that had been one of Chris's favorite foods as a small child. Now, because of his recent setbacks, it was one of the few foods he was capable of digesting.

Chris paused for dramatic effect, and then summoned all his breath to blow out the single birthday candle. "It may not sound like much," Barbara recalled, "but when you are on a ventilator, it takes great effort."

Two days later, Chris met with the production team for his animated film, *Everyone's Hero*. "He was extremely excited about it and very involved," said producer Ron Tippe. "Even when we asked if he wanted to take a break, he said, 'No, let's keep going.'"

On October 5, Chris appeared at a fund-raiser for the Rehabilitation Institute of Chicago. He met with doctors and patients, and promised that a cure for paralysis was near. "He electrified the crowd," said the institute's medical director, Dr. Elliot Roth. After the audience gave him a standing ovation, a tenor sang "The Impossible Dream."

Chris had shown no sign of illness or fatigue during his trip to Chicago. But the day after he returned to Bedford, nurses noticed that a sore on his lower back had become infected. For Chris, who had been fighting methicillan-resistant staphylococcus aureus (MRSA) for months, this meant heavier doses of the antibiotics he was already taking.

Dana knew that Chris pushed himself too hard, but she also trusted his judgment. No one knew his medical condition—what worked and what didn't—better than Chris. When she checked in with him on the phone, they did not dwell on this latest infection or what he was doing to treat it. Instead, she and Chris talked about the upcoming premiere of his film *The Brooke Ellison Story* at Manhattan's Lincoln Center. Dana also listened to Chris's plans to attend their son's hockey game and then spend the evening watching a Yankees–Minnesota Twins game on TV.

"Ah, more bonding," she said. "Sounds perfect."

"Yes," Chris replied before saying good-bye to Dana for the last time. "Perfect."

"Life is going to be full of pain,
but it doesn't have to be tragic.
And if you don't keep your sense
of humor, it can kill you."

—*Dana*

"The brightest light has gone out."

—*Robin Williams*

7

The pond Chris loved to gaze at for hours glistened in the pale yellow light of mid-October. While a string quartet played his favorite pieces by Mozart and Brahms, family and a few friends walked to the table that had been set up in the garden of the Bedford house. Each paused to place a single flower before a framed photo of Chris.

"It was one of the most beautiful New England days," Robin Williams said, "and leaves were turning and the wind's blowing and you're going, 'It feels like he's here, and that's a great thing.' There was a spirit of sadness but there's also a spirit of great joy all of a sudden."

When the service was over, the Reeve offspring began playing football. "It's what happens," Williams said. "Life goes on but that's what he'd want, too."

Two weeks later, nine hundred invited guests crammed into

the Juilliard Theater at Lincoln Center for a memorial tribute to Christopher Reeve. Glenn Close ("He is an irreplaceable force of nature. I will mourn him and celebrate him for the rest of my life."), Meryl Streep ("I thought of him all the time—when I had to go to work and get off my whiney-hiney, I thought of Christopher who never whined."), Robert Kennedy, Jr., and Iowa Senator Tom Harkin were among the many who spoke.

Will also came out onstage, and, speaking in a clear voice, said that his father "never faked it" and that he "lived to love." He recalled their last day together when Chris cheered him on at his hockey match, how they watched a Yankee game together, and how, when he kissed his father before going to bed, he had no way of knowing "it was the last time I would see him conscious."

There was audible sobbing in the audience during Will's remarks, which swelled as Dana spoke not only of her husband's courage and compassion, but of the little things that made him human. Among his quirks was to reply to "Hello" with "Hello to you," and "Good-bye" with "Good-bye to you." He "did not suffer fools gladly," she said, remembering the time they had gone to a play and the moment afterward when he announced: "Everybody can relax, the worst actor in the world has been identified."

She went on to speak of his love for his nurses and aides, of his "ironclad loyalty" to his friends, of the boundless pride he had for all three of his children. "I made a vow to Chris when we married that I would love him and I would be with him in sickness and in health," she concluded in a voice now choked with emotion. "And I did OK with that. But there's another vow that I need to amend today. I promised to love, honor, and cherish him until death did us part.

"Well, I can't do that," she went on, "because I will love, honor, and cherish him forever. Good-bye to you!" With that, Dana pulled away from the podium and fled the stage in tears.

Chris had, in fact, told Dana that when the time came, he wanted a party rather than a memorial service. For that, Dana said, she "apologized to his spirit. I said, 'I don't really much feel like having a party.' "

Yet she did go out of her way to invite the health care professionals who had cared for her husband over the years, and sought them out at the memorial service. "She made certain to come up to us and thank us personally," Kessler's Steve Kirshblum said. "She remembered the name of every doctor and nurse and aide. Dana was a total class act."

Kirshblum could also see that Will's speech had taken Dana by surprise. "Will really blew her away," he said. "For a young man to have such poise and courage—it was a credit to both his mom and his dad." Another guest, Brooke Ellison, agreed: "Will is precocious," she said. "Intimidatingly so. When you think of all he'd already been through . . ."

Not even Dana had been prepared for the outpouring of grief that followed news of Chris's death. George W. Bush and his opponent John Kerry put aside their bitter campaign for the White House to pay tribute to the man revered by millions around the globe. "Laura and I are saddened," said President Bush, who praised Chris as "an example of personal courage, optimism, and self-determination." Kerry lauded Chris as a "tireless champion for the disabled" who was "able to make great strides toward a cure without ever leaving his wheelchair."

In the following days and weeks, there would be questions

concerning the exact cause of Chris's unexpected death. But Dana did not request an autopsy. "I knew there was no reason," she explained. "He had the best care. The nurses and doctors had always got him through. If his body was failing, his body was failing." Chris's body was cremated, and his ashes scattered by the family.

Obviously too devastated to return to the Broadway cast of *Brooklyn Boy,* Dana called the play's author, Donald Margulies, to apologize. "Of course I understand," he replied. "Will just lost his father. It would be terrible if he had to deal with you being absent from his life."

Dana now focused on Will. The sudden death of his father was "a terrible, terrible shock," Dana said. But Will proved as resilient as his father—a testament to his upbringing. Will understood that "life has a lot of joy and laughter even amidst pain and hardship," she told her friend Larry King. "It's a life lesson I wouldn't have wished on him, but at the same time, he has coping skills a lot of twelve-year-olds might not."

Dana did not face some of the everyday problems widows often face; Chris's accident had forced her to become self-reliant. "Luckily, I really do understand the finances," she commented. "I know where the oil burner is, where the fuse box is."

But rather than being somewhat in the background when it came to her husband's efforts, she now dedicated herself to picking up where Chris left off. "Suddenly, I feel like I don't have a choice anymore. I have to carry on his mission."

Four days after her emotional eulogy for Chris, Dana officially stepped into his shoes as chairman of the Christopher Reeve Paralysis Foundation. Determined not to be just a figurehead, she insisted on reviewing every grant proposal and worked the phones lobbying senators and congressman just as Chris did. "Chris could be finessed," Peter Kiernan said. "Some people tried to take advantage of him. But nobody screwed with Dana. She was shrewd."

Her no-nonsense attitude in the boardroom notwithstanding, Dana brought an added personal touch to her dealings with foundation employees. "She was a very kind, warm person," one said. "She always called staff members by name and pulled up a chair so that she was never talking down to people in wheelchairs."

With help from the family—particularly her parents, Charles and Helen Morosini—Dana and Will managed to get through their first Thanksgiving and Christmas without Chris. But on January 20, 2005, Dana's dad called with the news that her mother had been diagnosed with ovarian cancer.

Dana was stunned. Coming so soon after Chris's death, Helen Morosini's illness seemed almost incomprehensible. However, Dana's can-do spirit quickly kicked in. She did some medical research of her own and, confident that her mother was getting the best medical care, went ahead with plans to attend President Bush's State of the Union address. There, seated in the gallery as a guest of Rhode Island Congressman Jim Langevin, she showed the flag in support of embryonic stem cell research.

Helen Morosini went into the hospital for surgery on February 6, and died from complications four days later—just three weeks after her initial diagnosis. She was seventy-one.

Dana was devastated. "A grinding ten-year fight? Dana was up for that," said Peter Kiernan. "But a fight that's over in a couple of weeks? That was a leveling blow."

Dana later remembered that her publishing executive mother

was, above all else, "a real mommy—a comfort and love. She was always there for me."

Helen Morosini's death was no less a shock for Will. "Will was *extremely* close to Helen," recalled their friend Becky Lewis. "She was a very strong presence in his life. She used to say, 'Will, you're a wonderment,' but she was a wonderment, too." For the next several months, he grieved over the sudden loss of his grandmother. As positive and resilient as he was, Dana admitted that her son was "reeling. It's a huge shock."

Dana would never get over either death. She would often tell friends that she wanted "more than anything" to pick up the phone and call her mother. With Chris, she was surprised to find that, months after his death, she was grieving about the accident all over again. "Wait a minute," she told herself, "I've done that."

Strangest of all were the times when she forgot he was gone altogether. On one out-of-town trip, Dana checked herself and Will into their hotel and then automatically headed for the phone. "Gotta call Daddy," she said brightly before reality struck. "Ooh . . ."

As she had done a thousand times before, Dana used the formula she had devised for coping with hard times—"When you least feel like it, do something for someone else." Soldiering on, she returned to Washington in April to lead a rally demanding increased funding for research into all forms of paralysis. A few weeks later, she helped promote a children's book inspired by her husband, *Dewey Doo-it Helps Owlie Fly Again,* and an accompanying audio version with Mandy Patinkin narrating and Dana and Bernadette Peters singing. Dana also had plans for a book of her own: That same month she signed a seven-figure deal with the Penguin Group to write about her relationship with Chris.

As the summer approached, Dana's life seemed to be turning a corner. "She was," her friend Michael Manganiello said, "excited about the future."

It was a future that included plans for a return to show business. That June, despite a persistent cough, Dana planned to relaunch her singing career with a two-night gig at Feinstein's, singer Michael Feinstein's posh nightclub in New York's Regency Hotel.

During rehearsals, Dana's coughing spells became so violent that she had to stop mid-song to catch her breath. When friends voiced concern, she assured them that she intended to consult her physician. "Yeah, I know," she said. "I just can't get rid of this thing. I'm going to get it checked out . . . Maybe next week."

On opening night, Dana somehow managed to banish the cough. For nearly two hours, she effortlessly glided through a selection of Broadway tunes and standards. Will, sitting in the front row with several of his cousins, beamed with pride.

"Chris was very much a part of the show," Michael Feinstein said. "Dana talked about him—about how they met and fell in love—and then she would sing . . . she seemed very strong and yet fragile at the same time. It was all very intimate and quite moving—people were crying—and there were moments when I felt I was intruding on something very private."

At one emotionally charged point in the show, she dedicated "I'll Be Seeing You" to Chris, and ended the song by blowing a kiss up to him. The evening ended with a standing ovation.

"You sensed," Feinstein recalled, "that she was embarking on a new life."

The cough that had been bothering Dana for weeks continued, and by July she was no longer willing to brush it off as the result of allergies or the flu. When she finally did visit the doctor, he ordered a chest X-ray. No one was prepared for what the X-ray revealed: a mass in one of her lungs.

"It was huge," she told her friend Kathie Lee Gifford. A biopsy and CAT scan confirmed that Dana, a lifelong nonsmoker, had advanced stage 4 lung cancer. Dana believed that at this point she had actually had the cancer for more than a year.

What she didn't realize, Dana told Gifford, was that lung cancer is in fact the number one killer among cancers. "I was always looking for breast, ovarian, and uterine," she said, "and you think, *I'm a nonsmoker and I live in the country, so I'm good.* So I am completely shocked." She speculated that perhaps her earlier years spent singing in smoky nightclubs might have been a factor— "but I guess I'll never really know."

After she broke the news to her father, Dana told him she was not really up to telling her younger sister, Adrienne. Once the news had time to sink in, Dana summoned the courage to speak with Adrienne. "It's a malignant tumor," she said before blurting out, "Oy vey!"

"It was funny," Adrienne later recalled. "But it wasn't."

The most important thing to Dana was finally knowing what was behind that nagging cough. "I'm glad to know the enemy," she said, "because now I can fight it."

What she dreaded most, of course, was breaking the terrible news to thirteen-year-old Will. She told him the tumor was inoperable, that she would probably have to undergo chemotherapy and perhaps radiation treatments—but that, in the end, she was determined to beat it. Kiernan described the conversation as "extraordinarily difficult for her. But Will's a smart boy and there was no point in sugarcoating it."

Dana made the point that she wanted Will to go on as usual with his life, and he did. "The kid is fantastic," she told Kiernan when he asked how he had taken the news of his mother's cancer. "It hasn't affected his schoolwork. It hasn't affected his hockey. I'm so proud of him."

Determined to keep news of her illness under wraps, Dana quietly began her chemotherapy treatments at New York's famed Memorial Sloan-Kettering Cancer Center. When she canceled plans to sing on the popular daytime program *The View,* Dana even kept the real reason a secret from the show's host, the Reeves' dear friend Barbara Walters.

Dana would not be able to keep the secret for long. When she learned that a tabloid was about to break the story, she reluctantly went public on August 9, 2005. Coincidentally, her announcement came just two days after the startling lung cancer death of ABC News anchorman Peter Jennings at age sixty-seven.

"I have an excellent team of physicians, and we are optimistic about my prognosis," she said in a statement. Then, displaying the sort of moxie she and Chris were so famous for, Dana added, "I hope before too long to be sharing news of my good health and recovery. Now, more than ever, I feel Chris with me as I face this challenge. As always I look to him as the ultimate example of defying the odds with strength, courage, and hope in the face of life's adversities."

On a certain level, Dana was relieved that the world now knew. "You know what?" she told one of Chris's oldest buddies. "I'm not going to hide."

Between chemo and radiation treatments, Dana continued to play an active role at the foundation she and her husband founded. By this time, it had distributed more than $55 million in research grants and nearly $9 million in the "quality of life" grants that Dana had championed for paralysis victims and their families.

Dana had also embarked on a new campaign, this time to raise awareness of lung cancer, which kills more women each year than breast, ovarian, and uterine cancer combined. "Did you know that?" Dana asked her friends. "Because I sure didn't."

"I never saw someone who could be so strong and positive," her friend Paula Zahn said, "in light of everything she went through." When Zahn asked where she got her energy, Dana replied, "Either I can sit here and wallow in self-pity or I can turn what we've gone through into something positive."

While only 5 percent of stage 4 lung cancer patients survive five years or longer, Dana's family and friends clung to the hope that she would be among them. That anyone who had already endured so much could be struck down so cruelly seemed incomprehensible.

Even as she fought the cancer with aggressive chemotherapy, Dana could still find humor in her situation. Calling Donald Margulies, Dana said, "Yeah, can you *believe* this?" She joked that she was losing her hair, but didn't have to "break out the Angelina Jolie wig just yet!"

To Peter Kiernan, she cracked in an email, "I've lost some

weight, but I can wear the jeans I used to wear in college and I look pretty good in them."

Dana proved it November 17, 2005, when she swept into the annual Christopher Reeve Foundation gala wearing a slinky gown, pearls, and Reeve Foundation dog tags bearing the Superman "S" logo. "The tumor is shrinking and shrinking and shrinking," she said.

Dana's physician dad was also optimistic. "The current strategy," he said, "is to turn it into a chronic disease. If we can manage to keep the cancer at bay then she can go on for years that way." But, he conceded, "it's still early in the game."

Whatever the outcome, Dr. Morosini was more in awe of his daughter than ever. "It's quite inspiring to see what she has had to deal with," her dad said. "She's a remarkable woman. She's taking on this latest challenge with grace, like she has done with everything else in her life." The American Cancer Society agreed. They named her Mother of the Year for her dedication to raising Will in the aftermath of her husband's death.

Charles Morosini had no idea that he would in fact be Dana's next unexpected challenge. While Dana played host to twenty-four members of the Reeve and Morosini families that Thanksgiving, her dad suffered a stroke in the middle of dinner and had to be rushed by ambulance to Northern Westchester Hospital.

Right away Dana pointed out that, since her house was already set up for handling people suffering from disabilities, she should take care of her father. "Her natural instinct was to have Dad move into her house," Adrienne said. The rest of the family convinced her that they could take care of Dad; she needed to focus on herself.

Charles Morosini would go on to make a complete recovery,

and it looked to the world as if Dana would, too. Although chemo had caused her hair to fall out, on January 12, 2006, she donned a wig to sing "Now and Forever" at a Madison Square Garden retirement ceremony for New York Rangers star Mark Messier. A friend of the Reeves', Messier occasionally gave Will hockey pointers when he and Dana dropped by after practice.

"It was a surprise and honor," Messier recalled when Dana appeared at the Garden. "You could just feel the energy from the crowd, it was so emotionally powerful." So powerful that she received a prolonged standing ovation. Later, Messier was even more moved to learn that Dana had actually changed her chemotherapy schedule to be there. "That," he said, "is the kind of person she was."

Later that month, the cancer began growing again. With Michael Manganiello at her side, Dana was shown new X-rays that clearly indicated the tumor had, in the doctors' words, "gone in a new direction."

Back in the hospital for more radiation treatment, Dana was still upbeat. She told everyone that she intended to go home, and proved her resolve to get better by never losing her sense of humor. "I'm beating the odds and defying every statistic the doctors can throw at me," she said in a group e-mail to her friends.

One of those friends, Mandy Patinkin, remembered one of her last e-mails. "She told us there was balance and fairness in this world," he said, "and she was going to be just fine."

By the end of February, Dana's condition had deteriorated rapidly—despite the fact that the cancer, according to Charles Morosini, was actually "in recession. But her lungs filled with fluid and she just went down. It took everybody by surprise."

On March 4, Dana summoned Peter Kiernan to the hospital. Without stating the obvious about her worsening condition, she told Kiernan she wanted him to take over as chairman of the foundation. "I told her," he said, " 'Civil rights leaders always have enemies, but the great thing was that you got to be a civil rights leader and everybody loves you!' "

At this point, family and friends rushed to the hospital to be by her side. But Dana wanted to hear funny stories. Even though her throat was seared from the radiation treatments and she could barely talk, she laughed through her pain when somebody brought up Groundhog Day. "I just thought," Adrienne recalled, "through this whole thing, she can barely swallow, and yet she kept her sense of humor. She was just a fighter."

Shortly after 10 P.M. on March 6, with her loved ones gathered around her, Dana slipped away. She was forty-four. "She was in high spirits to the end," said her father, Charles Morosini. "It was a very quiet passing, which gives you some comfort . . ."

Dana's entire family was at her bedside—with one glaring exception. "Will was not there," Charles Morosini said. "He didn't have the stomach for it."

Robin and Marsha Williams had visited Dana in the hospital, and had known that the end was near. Yet when word of Dana's death reached them, they both broke down. For once, Robin could only muster a few eloquent words. "The brightest light has gone out," he said. "We will forever celebrate her loving spirit."

Barbara Walters echoed the bewilderment felt by many of Dana's closest friends. "I was under the impression she was getting better," Walters said. "Then she was gone. I was devastated."

Indeed, as shocking as Christopher Reeve's death was, no one was prepared for this unexpected second blow. "Jack Kennedy once said life is unfair," observed their friend, playwright A. R. Gurney. "But this seems *brutally* unfair." Once again, world leaders, movie stars, and medical researchers alike joined in what amounted to a worldwide outpouring of dismay and grief. "Chris was America's superhero," John Kerry said, "and Dana became our hero, too." Another old friend, Larry King, said Chris and Dana "left us much too soon, but not before giving us two unforgettable profiles in courage."

Even as she was losing her valiant battle against cancer, Dana's thoughts were of Will and his future without a mom or dad. As unlikely a possibility as it seemed, she and Chris had both agreed some time ago that, if they were not in the picture, it would be better to have Will brought up by neighbors in familiar surroundings, rather than moved to live with relatives.

As his health began to fade in 2003, Chris revised his will to read, "If Dana shall fail for any reason to qualify as such Guardian hereunder . . . then I appoint my friends Robert Fraiman, Jr., and Nancy Fraiman."

Now that the unthinkable had happened, Will would move in with the family of a schoolmate—though not the Fraimans. "We were mentioned in Christopher's will initially," Nancy Fraiman explained, "but Dana wanted to place Will with a family where there were boys." One of the boys was Will's oldest friend. There was also a seventeen-year-old girl in Will's new family. This would enable Will to continue excelling at the school he had always attended, to play on the same teams alongside the same boys he grew up with, to flourish in the environment he had always known.

It was an arrangement that had the full approval of the Reeve and Morosini families, who would continue to play a large part in Will's life. "Same neighborhood, same friends," Charles Morosini said. "Everybody was happy with that."

"There's an embrace of family around Will," Peter Kiernan added. "The first circle is Matthew and Alexandra." (In fact, during Dana's last weeks, Alex had put her studies at Harvard Law School on hold to move into the Bedford house to care for Will.) Will would not be wanting for love—from his friends, from his family, and the countless people whose lives his parents touched.

Cycling legend and cancer survivor Lance Armstrong, who had befriended Dana and Will after Chris passed away, comforted Will two days after his mother's death. For a boy who had lost his father, his grandmother, and his mother in the span of seventeen months, Will was "showing the same courage his parents had," Armstrong said. In the coming weeks, Will and Armstrong would grow close. "I love hanging with him," Armstrong said. "I never thought I'd say that about a thirteen-year-old, but he's not your run-of-the-mill thirteen-year-old. He's a smart, well adjusted, mature, humble kid."

There was, as there had been for Chris, a small private funeral for Dana followed several weeks later by a star-studded memorial service—this time at Broadway's New Amsterdam Theater. The same people sat in the audience, this time sharing a look that fell somewhere between bewilderment and weary resignation. "It was beautiful," said Paula Zahn, one of more than nine hundred invited guests. "It was also raw. It was inspiring. It was heartbreaking."

"People were very much in a state of disbelief," added another guest, Brooke Ellison. "How could this happen to one family?"

For many the most touching moment came when sisters

Deborah and Adrienne sang a tune they often sang together with Dana as children—this time with a third voice, taking Dana's part, heard just offstage. "That brought the house down," Zahn said. "It was very, very sad and moving."

Once again Will, who arrived arm in arm with Matthew and Alexandra, stood up to pay tribute to a loved one—the mother who had taught him how to live and love in the face of soul-trying adversity. When he finished, the room erupted with applause. "Fortunately," observed family friend and neighbor John Bedford Lloyd, Chris and Dana "gave Will exactly what he will need—the gift of bravery and grace."

With Matthew, Alexandra, and Will carrying on the important work of their foundation, Chris and Dana left a truly unique legacy of caring, courage, and hope. None of it could have happened if Chris and Dana had not been true soul mates, the stars of one of the greatest true-life love stories of all time. In recognition of their equal partnership in life, one year after Dana's death the Christopher Reeve Foundation was renamed the Christopher and Dana Reeve Foundation.

Chris never doubted why their marriage—and their devotion to each other—endured. "Our love is built on a rock," he said, "like a lighthouse."

Toward the end, Dana found her mind drifting back to the beginning, when she was a hopeful young cabaret singer and he was Superman. "Suddenly I find myself missing the young Chris, missing the courting days, his whole being," Dana said wistfully. "I think he would like that."

ACKNOWLEDGMENTS

"He's got real potential," Kate Hepburn told me in 1976 when we spoke about the young man making his Broadway debut opposite her in Enid Bagnold's *A Matter of Gravity*. "Of course he'll have a lot more once I've kicked some sense into him!" It was classic Kate: She reserved such good-natured lambasting only for those she truly liked. And she truly liked Christopher Reeve.

But Hepburn, whose own love affair with Spencer Tracy became the stuff of legend, was in awe of Dana. She was more than just a loyal wife standing by her man; Dana displayed the kind of quintessentially American spirit that Kate admired above all else. "She never complains—you never hear either of them complain," Hepburn told me. "It's heartbreaking what's happened, but now we know they are just two damn extraordinary people, plain and simple."

Over the past thirty years, I have had the privilege of writing

about many famous couples. My books about Hepburn and
Tracy, Jack and Jackie Kennedy, Bill and Hillary Clinton, George
and Laura Bush, and Princess Diana examined the complex
forces that attract people to one another and then hold them together in the face of seemingly insurmountable odds. No story
was more poignant, yet ultimately more uplifting, than that of
Christopher and Dana Reeve.

A tremendous amount of research is essential for any com-
prehensive biography, and this was particularly true for this dual
biography of Christopher and Dana Reeve. In essence, work on
this book began when Kate Hepburn first introduced me to
Chris Reeve over thirty years ago—although no one could have
foreseen the strange twists in the road that would lead him from
playing a superhero to actually being one.

Many people spoke to me about how their lives had been
changed forever merely for having known Chris and Dana, but
none more movingly than Brooke Ellison. Brooke, who knows
something about courage and grace, had befriended the Reeves
when Chris directed *The Brooke Ellison Story* for television not long
before his death. "I'm honored to be a part of your book," Brooke
told me, echoing the sentiments of literally every one of the hundreds of people who I spoke to for *Somewhere in Heaven*. "The love
Chris and Dana had for each other—and the love they gave to
Will—was so powerful . . . They were an amazing couple, and it's
important for people to know that."

Once again, I have had the distinct privilege of working with
Hyperion's supremely gifted editor in chief Will Schwalbe—a
dear friend who is respected, admired, and genuinely liked
throughout an industry where personalities can often be, to put

it kindly, problematic. He is the proverbial Class Act. I also owe a debt of thanks to his consummately professional and eternally patient colleague, Brendan Duffy.

My thanks, as well, to all the folks at Hyperion—particularly Bob Miller, Ellen Archer, Will Balliett, Beth Gebhard, Phil Rose, Fritz Metsch, David Lott, Navorn Johnson, Muriel Tebid, and Chisomo Kalinga. I also owe a debt of gratitude to Camille McDuffie of Goldberg-McDuffie Communications, and to Brad Foltz for another superb cover design.

My agent, Ellen Levine, is another of those class acts that I've been fortunate enough to have in my life. No one is more passionate about books than Ellen, and no writer could ask for a more formidable advocate or a truer friend. In addition, my thanks to Ellen's talented colleagues at Trident Media Group, especially Claire Roberts, Alanna Ramirez, Adam Friedstein, Victoria Horn, and Melissa Flashman.

Chris and Dana Reeve put a high premium on family, and so do I. I was lucky to have two terrific parents—Edward and Jeanette Andersen—and lucky to be able to thank them in twenty-eight books. Our own daughters, Kate and Kelly, never cease to amaze us. They and their mother, Valerie, the source of their radiance and wit, make any complaints about life that I may have seem utterly trivial. Unlike Chris and Dana, Valerie and I have had the luxury of more than thirty-six years together—a testament to the fact that we, like the Reeves, were careful never to abandon our sense of humor.

Additional thanks to Peter Kiernan, Brooke Ellison, Dr. Steven Kirshblum, Dr. John Jane, Edward Herrmann, Senator Tom Harkin, Richard Matheson, Senator John Kerry, Ariel Dorfman,

A. R. Gurney, Dan Strone, Jack O'Brien, Dr. Patricia Morton, Erica Druin, Rebecca Lewis, Dr. Mo Nadkarni, William Baldwin, the late Katharine Hepburn, Charles Tuthill, Michael Frankfurt, Robin Bronk, Donald Margulies, Lendon Gray, Jennifer Van Dyke, Dr. Marcalee Sipski Alexander, the late John Houseman, Denise Richer, Dr. Oswald Stewart, the late Charlton Heston, Michael Feinstein, Richard Caplan, the late Joseph L. Mankiewicz, Jerry Pam, Ira Levin, Bill Diehl, Johnny Mandel, Jay Presson Allen, Annette Witheridge, Robbie Kass, Alicia Mohr, Diane Rosen, Enid Bagnold, Elene M., Robin Bowman, the late Sam Spiegel, Suzanne Morelle, David McGough, Shana Alexander, Don Cash Jr., Amy Beller, Tommy Cole, Lonny Chapman, Paula Dranov, the late Ellis Raab, Tom Freeman, Rosalind Halvorsen, James Watson, Amy Beller, Eugenia Szady, Ray Whelan Jr., Barrie Schenck, Kendra Day, Harry Benson, John Marion, Rosemary McClure, Lawrence R. Mulligan, Parker Ladd, Liz Richardson, Yvette Reyes, Dudley Freeman, Cranston Jones, Jennifer Prather, Lee Wohlfert, Gary Gunderson, James Bacon, Alfred Eisenstaedt, John Bryson, Elizabeth Loth, Tiffney Sanford, Julie Cammer, Mary Beth Whelan, Army Archerd, Liz Miller, the Christopher and Dana Reeve Foundation, the Kessler Institute for Rehabilitation, the Reeve-Irvine Research Center, the Juilliard School, Wesleyan University, Culpeper Regional Hospital, Northern Westchester Hospital, the University of Virginia Medical Center, South Coast Repertory, the Williamstown Theatre Festival, Cornell University, Middlebury College, the Bonnie J. Addario Lung Cancer Foundation, the New York Public Library, the staff of Motion Picture Study at the Academy of Motion Picture Arts and Sciences, Williams College, the New York Library of the

Performing Arts at Lincoln Center, the Creative Coalition, INSITE (the International Network of *Somewhere in Time* Enthusiasts), Talentworks, the Litchfield Business Center, CapedWonder.com, the Silas Bronson Library, the Gunn Memorial Library & Museum, the Brookfield Library, Reuters, the Associated Press, the *New York Times*, Associated Press/ Wide World, Sipa Press, Corbis, BEImages, Getty Images, and Globe Photos.

SOURCE NOTES

The following chapter notes are designed to give a general view of the sources drawn upon in preparing *Somewhere in Heaven*, but they are by no means intended to be all-inclusive. The author has respected the wishes of those interview subjects who have asked to remain anonymous and accordingly not listed here or elsewhere in the text. As a major international star following the release of his first Superman film in 1978, Chris was extensively covered by the Associated Press, Reuters, United Press International, and other major news agencies around the world. However, that paled in comparison to the tsunami of news stories triggered by his tragic accident in 1995. During the ensuing decade, Chris and Dana appeared in thousands of publications ranging from the *New York Times*, *USA Today*, *The Times* of London, the *Los Angeles Times*, the *Wall Street Journal*, and the *Washington Post* to *Time*, *Newsweek*, *People*, *Paris Match*, *Ladies' Home Journal*, *TV Guide*, *Esquire*, *Entertainment Weekly*, the *New Yorker*, *Parade*, *Good Housekeeping*, *Us*, *Readers Digest*, and *Vanity Fair*. Only a small representative sample of this coverage is offered here.

CHAPTERS 1 AND 2

Interview subjects and conversations with Edward Herrmann, Senator John Kerry, Peter Kiernan, Katharine Hepburn, Ariel Dorfman, Richard

Matheson, Jack O'Brien, Charles Tuthill, Donald Margulies, the late Charlton Heston, Jennifer Van Dyke, the late John Houseman, Johnny Mandel, the
late Francesco Scavullo, Ira Levin, James Bacon, Denise Richer, Enid Bagnold,
Cranston Jones, and Suzanne Morelle. Articles and other published sources
for this period included Douglas Martin, "Christopher Reeve, 52, Symbol
of Courage, Dies," the *New York Times*, October 12, 2004; Jim Fitzgerald,
"Superman Dies at 52," Associated Press, October 11, 2004; Joe Holley, "A
Leading Man for Spinal Cord Research," the *Washington Post*, October 11,
2004; Mark Hansel, "Christopher Reeve: Courage After the Cape," Associated
Press, October 11, 2004; Ann Oldenbury, "Superhero to the End," *USA To-
day*, October 11, 2004; Lisa Fleisher, Alison Gendar, Dave Goldiner, "Christo-
pher Reeve Taught People Two Words: Hope and Cure," the New York *Daily
News*, October 12, 2004; Roger Ebert, "He Showed Us The Real Hero,"
Chicago Sun-Times, October 12, 2004; Ken Regan as told to Alanna Nash,
"Remembering the Reeves," *Reader's Digest*, October 2006; Glenys Roberts,
"Superman to the Very End," the London *Daily Mail*, October 12, 2004; Bill
Hoffman, Cindy Adams, Valerie Perrine, Lou Lumenick, "America Hails
Christopher Reeve," the *New York Post*, October 12, 2004; Tom Gliatto, Saman-
tha Miller, Michelle Tauber, Jason Lynch, et al, "Heart of a Hero: Christopher
Reeve," *People*, October 25, 2004; Dirk Johnson, "A Job For Superman: The
Death of Christopher Reeve Leaves Embryonic Stem-Cell Activism Without
One of Its Star Generals," *Newsweek*, October 25, 2004; Joanna Powell, "Woman
of Steel," *Good Housekeeping*, August 1997; "On the Road to Movie Stardom,"
Blaine Harden, the *Washington Post*, March 13, 1977; Gene Siskel, "A Leader By
Inspiration," the *Chicago Tribune*, November 19, 1978; Vernon Scott, "A Serious
Actor Tackles the Man of Steel," United Press International, November 26, 1978;
Jack Kroll, "Superman to the Rescue," *Newsweek*, January 1, 1979; Kristin Mc-
Murran, "It's Superman!", *People*, January 8, 1979; Marguerite Michaels, "He
Insists He Can Act," *Parade*, June 27, 1982; Judith Michaelson, "Is There Life Af-
ter Superman?" the *Los Angeles Times*, August 20, 1984; Compton Miller, "Hap-
pily Unmarried," *The Sunday Times* of London, December 9, 1984.

CHAPTERS 3 AND 4

Information for these chapters was based in part on interviews and conversa-
tions with Dr. John Jane, Dr. Mo Nadkarni, Dr. Steven Kirshblum, A. R.
Gurney, Richard Matheson, Ariel Dorfman, William Baldwin, Michael
Frankfurt, Robin Bronk, Dr. Patricia Morton, Rebecca Lewis, Dr. Marcalee
Sipski Alexander, Dr. Oswald Stewart, Lendon Gray, Annette Witheridge,

James Watson, Jerry Pam, David McGough, Robin Bowman, John Bryson, and Erica Druin.

Published sources included Jeannie Park, Vicki Sheff-Cahan, "Eat Your Heart Out, Lois," *People*, April 20, 1992; Dave Zurawik, "Exit Superman, Enter a Shy Richard Collier," *Detroit Free Press*, August 12, 1979; Michael J. Bandler, "It Isn't Easy Being Superman!" *McCall's*, September 1987; Jerry Parker, "Christopher Reeve Leaps Beyond Superman," *Newsday*, August 12, 1984; Christine Arnold, "Christopher Reeve Tries to Shed Superman Image," the *Miami Herald*, January 18, 1981; Christopher Reeve, *Still Me* (New York: Random House, 1998); Patricia O'Hare, "He's Not Just Making 'Noises,'" the New York *Daily News*, April 8, 1992; Meredith Berkman, "Up, Out, and Away," *Entertainment Weekly*, November 5, 1993; Chris Nickson, *Superhero: A Biography of Christopher Reeve* (New York: St. Martin's Press, 1998); "Actor Hurt Horsing Around," the Associated Press, May 29, 1995; Kyle Smith, "Reel-Life Superman's Tale of Whoa," the *New York Post*, May 29, 1995; Linda Massarella, "Vigil for Superman: Family Gathers as Mystery Deepens Over Stricken Actor," the *New York Post*, May 31, 1995; Lois Romano, "Riding Accident Paralyzes Actor Christopher Reeve," the *Washington Post*, June 1, 1995; "Christopher Reeve, Thrown from Horse, Suffers Paralysis," Associated Press, June 1, 1995; Karen Freifeld, "Man of Steel Is Paralyzed," *New York Newsday*, June 1, 1995; George Rush, "Broken Dreams," New York *Daily News*, June 1, 1995; Linda Massarella, Lou Lumenick, Rita Delfiner, Kyle Smith, the *New York Post*, June 1, 1995; Lawrence K. Altman, "Actor Thrown from Horse Is Dependent on Respirator," the *New York Times*, June 2, 1995; Katy Kelly, "Reeve Doing Well After Surgery," *USA Today*, June 6, 1995; "Reeve's Spirits Are High After Surgery," Associated Press, June 7, 1995; Kendall Hamilton and Alden Cohen, "A Tragic Fall for Superman," *Newsweek*, June 12, 1995; Andrea Peyser, "Little Horse Sense Could Have Saved Superman: Trainer," the *New York Post*, June 12, 1995; Sandy Gonzalez, "Reeve's Steady Improvement Impresses Docs," the *New York Post*, July 12, 1995; Liz Smith, "Superman's Heartwarming Pledge: I'll Never Give Up," the *New York Post*, September 15, 1995; George Rush and Joanna Molloy, "Reeve's Laughter Contagious as Creative Types Turn Comics," the New York *Daily News*, October 18, 1995; Nadine Brozan, "'Superman' Star Is Back Before the Public," the *New York Times*, October 17, 1995; "Friends, Indeed," *People*, October 30, 1995; Kyle Smith, "Reeve Bares Own Brave Heart at Oscars," the *New York Post*, March 26, 1996.

CHAPTERS 5, 6, AND 7

For these chapters, the author drew on conversations with, among others, Peter Kiernan, Brooke Ellison, Dr. Steven Kirshblum, Michael Feinstein, Senator John Kerry, Michael Frankfurt, Senator Tom Harkin, Erica Druin, Donald Margulies, William Baldwin, Rebecca Lewis, Harry Benson, Dan Strone, Robin Bronk, Bill Diehl, and Jack O'Brien.

Michelle Green, "Love and Courage," *People*, April 15, 1996; Trip Gabriel, "Man of Steel Resolve: Christopher Reeve Champions Spinal Injury Research, Promises He'll Be 'Up and Around,'" the *New York Times*, April 16, 1996; Liz Smith, "We Draw Strength from Each Other," *Good Housekeeping*, June 1996; Roger Rosenblatt, "Super Man," *Time*, August 26, 1996; Lawrie Mifflin, "After a Life in Front of a Camera, A New One Behind It," the *New York Times*, October 13, 1996; Steve Daly, "A New Direction," *Entertainment Weekly*, November 15, 1996; Karen S. Schneider and Jane Shapiro, "Local Hero," *People*, January 27, 1997; Ileane Rudolph, "What She Does for Love," *TV Guide*, March 22, 1997; Todd Shapera, "Dana Reeve Makes Debut on Broadway," the *New York Times*, October 25, 1998; Adrian Havill, *Man of Steel: The Career and Courage of Christopher Reeve* (New York: Signet, 1996); Jeannie Williams, "Fall Breaks Reeve's Arm But Not His Spirit," *USA Today*, April 9, 1997; Howard Kissel, "Wife Has Super Job: Dana Reeve Sets Sights on a New Role," the New York *Daily News*, March 16, 1998; Denitia Smith, "A Life with a Before and an After," the *New York Times*, April 30, 1998; Chip Crews, "The Role He Can't Escape," *The Washington Post*, May 3, 1998; Nancy Shute, "Reeve's Super Struggle," *U.S. News and World Report*, May 11, 1998; Jeffrey Zaslow, "I Have to Give—Instead of Taking," *USA Today Weekend*, Mary 15, 1998; "Superman Star Vows Super Feat: Reeve Says He'll Walk in 5 Years," Reuters, June 1, 1998; "A Life Redefined," *Life*, November, 1998; Ileane Rudolph, "The Triumph of Christopher Reeve," *TV Guide*, November 21, 1998; Tom Carson, "Morbid Curiosity: Christopher Reeve Makes Hitchcock Uplifting in *Rear Window* Remake," the *Village Voice*, December 1, 1998; Christopher Reeve, *Nothing Is Impossible* (New York: Random House, 2002); Kevin O'Sullivan, "Robin Williams: Tears I Cried for Superman," the London *Mirror*, March 6, 1999; Melina Gerosa, "In Sickness and in Health," *Ladies' Home Journal*, November 1999; Dana Reeve, *Care Packages* (New York: Random House, 1999); Charles Krauthammer, "Restoration, Reality and Christopher Reeve," *Time*, February 14, 2000; Ellen Barry, "Christopher Reeve Urges Biotech Industry to Help Him Walk Again," Knight-Ridder/Tribune Business News, March 28, 2000; Christopher Reeve, "My Life Today," *Ladies' Home Journal*, August 2002; Andrew Walker, "Christopher

Reeve: Living in Hope," BBC News Profiles, March 1, 2002; Oliver Burke-man, "Man of Steel," *The Guardian*, September 17, 2002; G. Wayne Miller, "Christopher Reeve Makes His Case for Stem Cell Research," Knight-Rid-der, October 2, 2002; Paul Recer, "Christopher Reeve's Brain Can Function Normally If Spinal Cord Fixed," AP Worldstream, December 9, 2002; Sona Mark Kennedy, "Christopher Reeve's Wife Explores the Familiar Terrain of Heartache and Loss," AP Worldstream, September 26, 2003; Cal Fussman, "Christopher Reeve: What I've Learned," *Esquire*, January 2004; Sharon Churcher and Caroline Graham, "Farewell My Superman: The Grieving Mother of Christopher Reeve Talks for the First Time of Her Son's Courage as His Life Slipped Away," the London *Mail on Sunday*, October 17, 2004; CNN Transcript, "Remembering Christopher Reeve," *Larry King Live*, October 17, 2004; Lisa Birnbach, "Do Something for Someone," *Parade*, May 1, 2005; Jim Fitzgerald, "Christopher Reeve's Wife Has Lung Cancer," Associated Press, Au-gust 9, 2005; Chip Crews, "Dana Reeve Gets Diagnosis of Lung Cancer," the *Washington Post*, August 10, 2005; Jim Fitzgerald, "Christopher Reeve's Widow Dies at Age 44," Associated Press, March 7, 2006; Nadine Brozan, "Dana Reeve, 44, Devoted Caretaker and Advocate, Is Dead," the *New York Times*, March 8, 2006; Adam Bernstein, "Dana Reeve: Widow Advocated for Paralysis Re-search," the *Washington Post*, March 8, 2006; Jim Smolowe, Fannie Weinstein, Sharon Cotliar, Mary Green, Sean Scully, Sandra Marquez, and Alicia Dennis, "Dana Reeve: Brave to the End," *People*, March 27, 2006; Ryan Parry, "Su-permum's Final Act of Love," the London *Mirror*, May 25, 2006.

SELECTED BIBLIOGRAPHY

Bellomo, Michael. *The Stem Cell Divide: The Facts, the Fiction, the Fear Driving the Greatest Scientific, Political, and Religious Debate of Our Time*. New York: AMACOM, 2006.

Dorfman, Ariel. *Death and the Maiden*. New York: Penguin, 1994.

Dougan, Andy. *Robin Williams: A Biography*. New York: Thunder's Mouth Press, 1999.

Ellison, Jean and Brooke Ellison. *The Brooke Ellison Story: One Mother, One Daughter, One Journey*. New York: Hyperion, 2004.

Havill, Adrian. *Man of Steel: The Career and Courage of Christopher Reeve*. New York: Signet, 1996.

Holland, Suzanne, Karen Lebacqz, and Laurie Zoloth, editors. *The Human Embryonic Stem Cell Debate: Science, Ethics, and Public Policy*. Cambridge, Massachusetts: The MIT Press, 2001.

Houseman, John. *Final Dress*. New York: Simon & Schuster, 1983.

Leaming, Barbara. *Katharine Hepburn*. New York: Crown, 1995.

Matheson, Richard. *Bid Time Return*. New York: Viking Press, 1975.

Nickson, Chris. *Superhero: A Biography of Christopher Reeve*. New York: St. Martin's Press, 1998.

Reeve, Christopher. *Still Me*. New York: Random House, 1998.

————. *Nothing Is Impossible: Reflections on a New Life*. New York: Random House, 2002.

Reeve, Dana. *Care Packages: Letters to Christopher Reeve from Strangers and Other Friends*. New York: Random House, 1999.

Reeve, Franklin D. *The Toy Soldier and Other Poems*. Calgary, Alberta: Bayeux Arts, 2007.

Scavullo, Francesco. *Scavullo on Men*. New York: Random House, 1977.

Somers, Martha Freeman. *Spinal Cord Injury: Functional Rehabilitation*. New York: Prentice-Hall, 2001.

Switzer, Jacqueline Vaughn. *Disabled Rights: American Disability Policy and the Fight for Equality*. Washington D.C.: Georgetown University Press, 2003.

INDEX

Peters, Bernadette, 206
Petri, Jim, 57–58
Pinochet, Augusto, 46, 47, 48
Portraits, 192
Practice, The, 191
Pretty Woman, 56–57
Proprietor, The, 79
Psacharopoulos, Nikos, 20, 22

Quest for Camelot, The, 162

Raffin, Deborah, 65
Reagan, Nancy, 181
Rear Window, 178–79
Redford, Robert, 30
Reeve, Alexandra (daughter), 36,
    39, 40, 61, 69, 72–74, 102,
    144, 146, 159, 177, 194, 196,
    215, 216
  birth of, 35
  Chris's accident and, 95, 96, 98
  Chris's death and, 7
  and Chris's romance with Dana,
    44, 46, 48–49
Reeve, Alison (Chris's half-sister),
    24
Reeve, Barbara, *see* Johnson,
    Barbara
Reeve, Benjamin (Chris's brother),
    8, 24, 25, 70, 96, 102–3
Reeve, Brock (Chris's half-brother),
    24
Reeve, Christopher:
  as airplane pilot, 31, 35, 36, 62,
    76
  appendectomy of, 38
  on balloon ride, 35
  birth of, 23–24
  causes supported by, 59, 60, 73,
    76–77, 87, 136
  childhood of, 25–26
  costs of care for, 139, 139, 142,
    165, 185, 194–95

Dana's marriage to, 68–70
Dana's meeting of, 13–17, 40
Dana's romance with, 40–46, 50
death of, 9, 204
feeling and motion regained by,
    173, 187–88, 189
fiftieth birthday of, 189–90
film debut of, 29
funeral service for, 201
horse allergy of, 25, 33–34, 37,
    55, 75
horseback riding of, 37–38,
    54–55, 71–72, 74–76, 79–80,
    87–91
horseback riding accident of, 8,
    91–112, 146–47, 158, 168,
    175, 176
horse sold by, 146
malaria contracted by, 76
marriage feared by, 23, 35–36,
    64–67, 185
medical setbacks suffered by, 4,
    6–9, 115–17, 145, 172–73,
    174, 182, 186–87, 193–94,
    195, 197
memoirs of, 122, 142, 176
memorial tribute to, 201–3
parasailing accident of, 36–37
physical therapy of, 126–27,
    145, 175, 186, 187, 188,
    189, 193
sailing of, 45, 55–56, 62, 65, 86,
    167–68
sex life of, 158–61
soap opera role of, 27–28
spirituality of, 185–86
stage career of, 13–14, 18, 20,
    26–27, 28–29, 34–35, 40, 49,
    53, 58–59
as Superman, 15, 29–31, 32, 34,
    35, 38, 47, 48, 60, 76, 77,
    135–36, 169
tax debt of, 58

Reeve, Christopher *(continued)*
  television work of, 27–28,
    57–58, 59, 80–81, 191, 193
  ventilator of, 108–9, 127–28,
    131, 134, 138, 145, 178, 181,
    184, 191
  wheelchair of, 117, 118, 127,
    132–33, 134, 143
Reeve, Dana:
  birth and childhood of, 18–19
  cancer of, 207–12, 214
  causes supported by, 73, 76–77
  Chris's accident and, 92–112
  Chris's death and, 9
  Chris's marriage to, 68–70
  Chris's meeting of, 13–17, 40
  Chris's romance with, 40–46, 50
  death of, 213–14
  funeral and memorial service for,
    215–16
  in high school, 19–20
  horseback riding of, 19, 54, 55,
    175
  pregnancy of, 67–68, 69, 70
  sailing of, 45, 55–56, 62, 86,
    167–68
  sex life of, 158–61
  singing of, 13, 18, 19, 21, 45, 96,
    171, 175–76, 207, 212
  stage career of, 13–14, 17–18,
    20–21, 153–54, 179–80, 192,
    196
  television work of, 165–66, 183,
    192
Reeve, Franklin "F.D." (Chris's
    father), 23–25
  Chris's death and, 8
  Chris's Superman role and,
    29–30
Reeve, Mark (Chris's half-brother),
    24
Reeve, Matthew (son), 36, 39, 40,
    61, 69, 72, 73–74, 102, 144,

  146, 159, 177, 189, 190, 194,
    215, 216
  Chris's accident and, 95, 96, 98
  Chris's death and, 7, 8
  and Chris's romance with Dana,
    44, 45, 46, 48–49
  birth of, 34
Reeve, William (son), 5–6, 8, 72,
    74, 78, 80, 87, 89, 90, 114,
    115, 116, 118–22, 129, 138,
    139, 143–45, 154, 159, 160,
    162, 166, 172, 173 177–78,
    181, 189, 190, 192, 194–96,
    211, 214–15
  birth of, 71
  Chris's accident and, 92–95, 99,
    101–2, 104–7, 184, 194
  Chris's death and, 6–7, 9, 204,
    215
  Dana's illness and death and,
    208–9, 213, 215
  Helen Morosini's death and, 206,
    215
  hockey played by, 4–5, 212
  at memorial tribute for Chris,
    202, 203
  at memorial tribute for Dana,
    216
Reeves, George, 30
Regan, Ken, 35, 125–26
Rehabilitation Institute of Chicago,
    196–97
Reid, Lisa, 90–91
Remains of the Day, The, 71, 72, 73,
    77, 79, 150
Richer, Denise, 14
Roberts, Deborah, 183, 184
Roosevelt, Franklin, 138, 169–70
Rosenblatt, Roger, 169
Ross, Herb, 167
Roth, Elliot, 197
Rover, The, 14, 16, 40, 43
Rudolph, Ileane, 168